Discovering Our Born-Again Identity

Becoming More Conscious of
The Greater One Living
Within Us

Gloria Kramer

PRESS

Dedication

This book is gratefully dedicated to
JESUS.
He is the lover of my soul and my very best
friend.

Table of Contents

Foreword

It was a joy for me to read the pages of this book. For me it was not just a story of someone's life and growth, but it was a real life person in whom I have believed, prayed for, and invested greatly. The joys and sorrows along with the struggles and victories you are about to read are real.

I met Gloria in the fall and winter of 1986 as we worked together on a community evangelistic event. I was impressed with her walk with Christ then. About a year later, as the Lord led my wife and I out of our traditional church to plant a full gospel church, the Lord also led Gloria and her family to be one of the founding members of our church.

I quickly began to work closely with and learn from Gloria. The Lord had told us that He wanted this church to have a strong foundation in prayer. I did many things to facilitate that into reality. Gloria was a foundation piece as she lived her heart and ministry as a true intercessor. Joyfully, I recall serving in childcare to allow the women to pray unhindered and uninterrupted. Gloria's children were among them and how I love those kids (now grown). I still believe and trust that Gloria is a God called intercessor.

The growth in Gloria continued as we prayed together as a church and watched God grow vital ministries to reach people. I recall a day early in the life of the church when I was praying for God to raise up a ministry to women. As I devoted myself to focused intercession for this, the Lord gave me the leading to choose Gloria. He showed me a vision of her standing and ministering the Word of God before thousands of people in a large stadium. That same day, the Lord brought Gloria across my path, and I shared it with her. The tears began to flow as she revealed the calling from the Lord even as a young girl to preach the gospel of Christ. That day, a process to disciple and help her prepare for the call began. She served the Lord through our church in so many ways, but growth, wisdom, and anointing has been the outcome. I am so glad that I have been able to serve her as a "Barnabas" to encourage and aid her in her pursuit of His call.

As the years passed, the Lord moved me from close geography to Gloria and her family. While I was very supportive in her ministry, much time had passed without having the privilege of sitting under her ministry. In early 2002, a time of deep stress and crisis in her personal life, she came to minister at our present church. I was so overwhelmed by the powerful anointing and authority in Christ that flowed from her ministry. The gift of God upon her to transform lives was real. I stand as a witness in praise to the Lord at work in and through Gloria.

Now this book, coming from God at work in her life, is going to powerfully touch your life. Make your heart open. Let the Lord have His way!

Pastor John Thomas
Peru, Indiana

Endorsements

"I believe this work was done under the inspiration of the Holy Spirit, and that it will serve to benefit the body of Christ. Many Christians need to read this material."

Pastor Joseph "Gary" Beaton
Assembly of God Tabernacle
Christiana, Jamaica

"It is fantastic . . . we are so glad you are ministering through this book at this time in which we live . . . very timely. We pray that God will richly bless those that read it and set many free to find their identity in Christ."

Daniel & Delia Hale
Rivers of Living Water International, Inc.
Alexandria, Louisiana

"I liked the book and was impressed with the manner in which you expressed yourself and I believe it will bless the lives of a lot of people."

Charles Thompson
Jesus Is Lord Ministries
Heber Springs, Arkansas

Acknowledgments

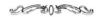

I would like to thank and acknowledge my four children who had to witness and live with my identity crisis. I know you were greatly affected by my *process* of transformation but someday I hope you will be able to say it was worth it.

For any pain that may remain, I pray the Lord Jesus will heal you.

On the other hand, this is what life is: A journey. Unfortunately, you were not able to choose whether you wanted to come along. It was assigned to you. It would not have been the same without each of you but instead it has been exactly what God intended. I will always be eternally grateful.

Although this *process* has been slow, and at times seemingly stopped, thank you for not giving up on me. Your unconditional love for me was so undeserved and yet so appreciated. My greatest desire is that the truths from these pages will help you discover your own born-again identity. I wish I had them before you were a part of my life.

Sometimes life is not fair but unfairness does not have to defeat you. When given to God, He can use it to His advantage. He can and will rebuild you and empower you to be better rather than bitter.

For the times you want to quit, please remember that anyone can quit. It takes a personal relationship with Jesus to keep going. Nothing else in this world can compare with it, and nothing else in this world can take His place.

Remember that we are all still works in progress.

> *Being confident of this very thing, that He who has begun a good work in you will complete it until the day of Jesus Christ.*
>
> (Philippians 1:6)

> *He who calls you is faithful, who also will do it.*
>
> (1 Thessalonians 5:24)

Through all the hardship of the past few years, I regret that you had to experience so much pain. By far, the greatest identity crisis and reshaping has taken place in the last few years due to your dad and me separating. I am so very proud that you are evolving from this family separation and I trust that you will find Jesus is faithful. I love you and nothing will ever change that!

Mark, I am in the ministry today because of your support. I wanted to quit so many times, but you continually encouraged me. Your support enabled me to be a stay at home mom and gave me the opportunity to go to Bible College. I appreciate that gift.

Mom, your support and prayers have enabled me to remain in the ministry. I know your reward will be great in Heaven. Just as you have done it for me, you have done it for the Lord.

I also lovingly acknowledge my father, Louis Mullen, who has already made his entrance into heaven. He taught me to be myself and that it was okay to be different. I miss him!

To all my family, friends and my church family who have endured me: Thank you. I pray that the Lord will richly bless you.

And to all the ministers the Lord chose to "cross" my path, I thank you for obeying the Holy Spirit. I am a life that was changed. Some plant, some water, but it is God who gives the increase.

Pastor John, thank you for writing the foreword of this book and for believing in me and encouraging me to answer the call of God.

I want to also acknowledge my Aunt, Mary Ann McKim, who eagerly began editing this manuscript. Her enthusiasm and encouragement served to be a tremendous motivation for me. She went home to be with the Lord before the book was complete. I know she heard the Lord say "Well done!"

And lastly, I want to acknowledge and thank my cousin Linda Mullen Clevenger and Anissa Martin for your help in editing this manuscript and for all your writing tips. The Lord is not unjust to forget your labor of love.

Author's Note

Having had this book professionally edited by two very talented ladies, I chose to leave some of the things as they were written for the purpose of simply being me. By doing this, you may not always find writing accuracy but you will find the vulnerability of an open heart. Perhaps the words of Paul will say it best:

> *For I resolved to know nothing (to be acquainted with nothing, to make a display of the knowledge of nothing, and to be conscious of nothing) among you except Jesus Christ (the Messiah) and Him crucified. And my language and my message were not set forth in persuasive (enticing and plausible) words of wisdom, but they were in demonstration of the [Holy] Spirit and power [a proof by the Spirit and power of God, operating*

> *on me and stirring in the minds of my*
> *hearers the most holy emotions and*
> *thus persuading them]. . .*
> (1 Corinthians 2:2, 4, Amplified)

After all, it is not by might nor by power that things are accomplished, but by the Spirit of the Lord.

My trust in the Holy Spirit far exceeds my inabilities. It is my conviction that the Holy Spirit gives life. It is my prayer that He gives life to the reading of this work for His honor and glory!

Gloria Kramer

Introduction

This book was written because I felt the Holy Spirit asked me to. I really didn't know how to write a book and I tried to tell Him so, but it was as if He was asking me to just trust Him. His prompting and direction have made it a reality. I realize it was being written everyday in my heart but now the words are written on these pages.

This book is about my journey to find my identity; something I struggled with all my life. I believe that much of the world is struggling with an identity crisis. The bleaker picture is that much of the body of Christ is in an identity crisis as well. The Lord wants this to change.

Many things form our identity: Our parents, siblings, friendships and other countless relationships along the way contribute to our understanding of who we are. Circumstances also have a tremendous impact on the type of person we become especially those which are out of our control. Loneliness, neglect, and lack of purpose emerge when busy parents and role models do not realize their responsibility in molding our identity.

Generation after generation, identities continue to be crippled. Some people can't figure out who they are or what they have been created to do and because we have had little leadership or guidance, we have accepted the lie that *this* is an acceptable way of life.

People are climbing corporate ladders hoping that fulfillment is found at the top only to find that once they reach there, they are still empty and unsure of who they really are.

As a minister, I see the struggle of individuals trying to find purpose and fulfillment in their life. I witness failure in the lives of Christians because they simply did not know their born-again identity. There is a battle between truth and deception, worthiness and unworthiness. The reality of the Word of God gets lost in overwhelming appetites for emotional dominance and acceptance. I have seen that a continual circle of bad choices bring only death and destruction. A circle some never seem to escape. The purpose of Jesus is to bring life and life abundantly (John 10:10).

Christians are turning to drugs, alcohol, dieting, overeating, popularity, control, pornography, abortion, moral failure, and even suicide to fill the emptiness inside. The reason for this is they believe a lie rather than the truth. Yet the Word of God tells us that *life* . . . the very life of Christ . . . resides in us! My desire is to expose these lies of the enemy, lies that are convincing Christians to turn to other things rather than to the Lord. Lies that tell us Jesus is not enough when we know that the Bible tells us we are complete in Him. My purpose is to bring light to the above areas of darkness that bring people into deception. This deception is robbing the people of God from their born-again destiny.

The passion of my heart is to reveal some of the truths that God has shown me over the years. I want to share some of the principles that I have used to overcome the enemy's strategy of paralysis. I pray you will find yourself in these pages.

The plan of God is life! The purpose of God is victory! The pursuit of man is pleasing God by fulfilling our God-ordained destiny. To fulfill our destiny, we must know who He has created us to be.

Jeremiah 29:11 states, *"For I know the plans I have for you, declares the Lord, plans to prosper you and not harm you, plans to give you a hope and a future."*

No matter what your background, your childhood, the wrong choices you have made in the past, God has a plan and it is a good plan. It is God's desire that you overcome the past. He wants to saturate your life with His presence and glory, and illuminate your future.

I pray the Holy Spirit will use this book to bring hope, strength, and encouragement. You *can* find your born-again identity.

"Where you are, is not where you are going.
And where you have been, is not
where you have to stay!"
The Holy Spirit

Chapter 1

The Journey Begins

As a girl growing up, I was the oldest of five daughters. For as long as I can remember, I felt somehow God had made a mistake in making me a girl. I wasn't interested in the things that interested other girls. My earliest childhood indication of a future identity crisis occurred when I was five. My mother found me outside without my shirt. When she tried to explain to me that girls had to wear shirts, I replied, "The boys don't have to wear any." Thus my journey began to learn who I was.

Growing up was hard. I was taller than other girls and boys my age. I didn't seem to fit anywhere. Most of my friends and neighbors were boys and I liked doing the things they did. You would find me in the ditches hunting crawl dads, roaming the underground sewers, climbing trees, or playing tag football in our backyard.

Dad gave me the responsibility of mowing our yard with the riding lawn mower. The first time I tried, I didn't know that after I put it in reverse, I was to let go of the clutch. As you can imagine, I found myself and the mower in the ditch and I had to call for my dad's help. At times I felt I could not measure up to his expectations.

Some of my fondest memories spent with my dad are going fishing and hunting mushrooms. He also taught me how to pitch horseshoes and washers, and play cards. Everything with dad was a competition. He was good at everything he put his hand to accomplish. Other memories include how he taught me to shoot a rifle, skin squirrels, and filet fish. He taught me how to drive a car and because he was an avid bowler, he taught me a thing or two about that as well. Being the oldest girl in the family and having no sons, I tried to be the son my dad didn't have and I tried to win his approval.

I was interested in sports and played softball, volleyball, basketball, and ran track. I didn't do too badly in the classroom either. I was an honor roll student and for every A on my report card, dad would give me a dollar.

Apart from being hang-out friends, I wasn't very interested in boys. At first I was too busy, but as most girls eventually learn, the day came when I became aware of boys. This caused problems between my dad and me because he didn't want me to grow up. Because my mother understood, she was my savior. She became a mediator between us.

A Childhood Encounter

It would be appropriate to insert here, that as a child I had an unusual curiosity about the Lord. I have always had a love for the Lord. As a young girl, I would lie outside at night under the stars and wonder where God was. Was He looking down on me? What would it be like to be with Him? As a child though, He seemed far away.

I tried many times to draw near to Him. I especially related to God in nature. Being in a busy household of girls, it was sometimes hard to find some quiet personal space.

At the young age of ten, I made a personal decision to accept Jesus into my heart. I walked the aisle of the church and sensed that somehow I had been united with a long distance relative. I was baptized in water and felt that God had a purpose for my life.

Some of the other girls and I in the church formed a quartet, traveled to various singing competitions and won several trophies. Our favorite song was titled, "I've got a Mansion Just over the Hill Top." I also received several awards from church camp, like the "camper of the week." Many of these awards were based on points earned for memorizing the scriptures.

One particular hot summer day, I was sitting on our back porch when it began to rain. At that moment in time, I felt so close to the Lord. I began to praise Him from the depths of my being. Words to songs I did not know flowed from my heart. Love songs.

Worship songs. I would find out later the Bible calls them "new songs".

On this day, I had a vision. I didn't know what "a vision" was, but I knew I had *seen* something. It would be seventeen years later before I would tell anyone. In the vision, I saw myself standing before multitudes of people as far as my eye could see.

They were people of different nations, men, women, boys and girls. It startled me and I wasn't sure what I was to do with it. Like Mary, I just pondered it in my heart for many years. I was really unaware of it at the time, but God was leading me and actually calling me into the ministry. I was in a denominational church that taught that God didn't use women, so it was to be mine and the Lord's secret.

Many times at night when I would lay my head down on the pillow, I would ask God to forgive me of anything I had done wrong. I wanted things to be right just in case it would be my last night.

This church where I had walked down the aisle to be saved had become a family to me. I had many close friendships there. I spent many nights with this dear elderly couple. They took me in and bought me gifts. They cared about my family and would visit my parents to witness to them. It was a happy time in my life.

A Turning Point

The next few years would bring many disappointments. Eventually, the pastor of the church had an affair and left. People seemed to scatter including me. I began to attend my grandmother's church until my Sunday school teacher began to act inappropriately, making me feel uncomfortable. I would understand later that he had a spirit of lust. I found myself running again.

My best friend began to experiment with a new lifestyle. Her parents were going through a divorce and she was frequently left unsupervised at her grandmother's house. She got into the wrong crowd and began smoking. I still remember the day she showed me the cigarettes in her dresser drawer. I was heart broken because she too had made a decision to accept Jesus but now she was turning away. Along the way, we grew apart and once again I found myself alone. One of my sisters also began to follow the wrong crowd and for a time befriended my now distant friend. It hurt when they came around the house together.

It seemed that many of my church role models and friends were running from God when I wanted to run toward Him.

A Love Encounter

Many times my mother would send me to a local hang out to get my sister. It was there that I would meet my husband. He would flirt with me but at first I pretended not to be interested. I actually looked down on most of the people there. I perceived them to be hoods. I did not want to be in a group of trouble makers.

Over time I began to fall for Mark, my future husband. On his nineteenth birthday, he asked me if I would give him a birthday kiss. I didn't answer at first. As circumstances would have it, the kiss did take place. A few weeks later he was to leave for basic training. He had enlisted in the United States Army! We had just met, he couldn't be going away, but he did. We stayed in touch with letters and phone calls. He confessed that he was falling in love with me and wanted me to be his wife. A year and one month after that kiss, we were married. Not only were we married, but I was pregnant.

From the young age of ten, the time of the vision, until the still young age of 17, many circumstances and decisions were made that seemed to take me far away from standing before multitudes of people for God. What do I do now, Lord?

During a complicated delivery I called out to the God of my childhood and said, "Lord, I have made so many mistakes and I am not sure how I got here, but please help me."

Our son was born while Mark was on a 30 day leave before reporting for duty in Seoul, Korea for a thirteen-month tour. Thirteen months seemed like eternity. I was now alone again and not sure where to go.

A Year to Grow Hungry

During the year I stayed busy raising my son and going back to school. I took night classes and got my GED.

Mark returned from Korea in April of 1982 and while we waited for his discharge date in October, we rented a small house. It was looking like we might finally be able to start our lives together.

Mark's brother-in-law invited us to a Full Gospel Business Men's Meeting in Evansville, IN. We accepted and that night I felt the love and presence of God like I had felt that rainy summer afternoon so many years before.

Afraid of what Mark would think, I did not respond to the altar call that night. I was well aware that the Lord was calling me *again*. Later that night Mark could not sleep and asked me if I was awake. I told him that I was and he began to ask me what I thought of the meeting. We both confessed that we wanted to go forward and receive Jesus so we asked Him into our hearts right then and there. It was a precious and glorious moment. I was so thankful that we were deciding to serve the Lord together. This was the perfect start to a new beginning.

I found that the call of God was still there after all those years and after all those mistakes. In October 1982, I was baptized in the Holy Ghost. My life would change forever!

A New Life

Like most young Christians, our new life in Christ was met with many hardships, trials, and reasons to quit. Right after surrendering our lives to the Lord, Mark lost his job. We could barely make ends meet but it was our conviction that I would be a stay at home mom. I began to ponder the question, "Why am I here and what am I to do with my life?"

I began to seek the Lord for the answer but I was not expecting what He was to show me. He began to deal with my heart about forgiving Mark for getting me pregnant. I blamed him for my lost dreams and goals but the Lord was telling me I had to take responsibility for my own actions. In the same way He had forgiven me, I had to forgive Mark. Soon after this revelation my life began to take new direction. The Lord seemed to be ordering my steps and I found myself moving forward in the things of God.

The Billy Graham Association brought the movie "Cry from the Mountain" to our area and I was asked to be a part of the advertising team where I would meet my future pastor. It was exciting to be a part of something God was doing.

I also began to attend a Charismatic prayer group where I was quickly asked to do some teaching. Not long after I started attending, they decided to make me a core leader.

Through the gifts of the Holy Spirit words were coming forth about my future, words involving "healing," "responsibility," and a "prophetic ministry." Who me, the housewife from Indiana, high school drop-out, and pregnant teen-age statistic? My new life in Christ was beginning to take shape. I was starting to see that God was training me and that He had use of me.

Molding the Clay

Desire to serve the Lord was pulsating through me. He was giving me more responsibility and I was growing. I was learning new and exciting things all the time. The Lord was allowing me to meet new people, attend crusades, and healing conferences. And many prayers were being answered.

A lady attending the prayer meeting had asked for prayer concerning a lump under her arm about the size of a golf ball. I prayed for her and the lump shrank and disappeared.

Insight and understanding about people I did not know began to operate in my life. It was as if the Lord had me on His potter's wheel and was molding me into a completely different person. At times, I was surprised by the things the Lord did through me. This was a time in my life where I was beginning to see the awesome power of God demonstrated.

I was being stretched and challenged to believe Him for more. We were seeing some fantastic things happening in our personal life as well. The Lord was blessing financially and meeting our needs supernaturally. It was a time of learning experientially that God could be trusted.

I was enjoying the opportunities I had to teach in this prayer group but yet there was this undefined desire for more . . . for something else.

A Divine Appointment

As already mentioned, I met my pastor working on the Billy Graham movie. A couple of years later, he was starting a new church and invited our family to be a part of this new beginning. The Lord spoke to my heart and said, "Jump in with both feet." I did not understand at the time that it was a divine appointment.

It was here in this little church that I would cut my teeth so to speak. I first started out as a volunteer in the office. I began to move into intercessory prayer asking God to bring increase to the church. I wept many tears in prayer for that church in its infancy. They were small beginnings but very valuable.

I am so thankful for my pastor. He gave me many opportunities to serve and grow. Eventually, he would invite me to be the Women's Ministry leader. The Holy Spirit allowed him to see something in me. Many times he went to bat for me defending my sincerity because people would misunderstand my passion.

The truth is, many times I did not move with a lot of wisdom, but I did have a lot of zeal and my heart was in the right place. I am so thankful that the Holy Spirit allowed him to see what others could not see.

God really began to teach me who I was in Christ.

Beginning Identity Training

Through the responsibilities of leading a women's ministry at the church, I felt I was making a difference. The Lord was moving, the ladies were growing, and lives were being touched. It was very rewarding to be working in the kingdom.

Two years later I would encounter a major reshaping of my identity. The Lord was speaking to me that it was time to step down, but "Women's Ministry Leader" was *my* identity. What would I be if I resigned? I would just be a housewife from Indiana, high school drop-out, pregnant teen-age statistic again. My response to the Lord was, "No! I can't let it go." I did not know the Lord wanted to promote me.

True identity begins when you can let go of what you hold the tightest. I had to let go of my insecurities and fears. True identity can come when you are secure enough to obey God.

The Lord graciously sent two wonderful ladies to our church from Davenport, Iowa. I met privately with them and they began to ask some very hard questions. By the time they were done with me in that meeting, I was a mess, but I also knew what I had to do.

The Lord had already given me the name of my replacement and that alone was a hurdle. Who wants to be replaced? No one does. The other woman and I were becoming good friends. I had confidence in her. This was not about her ability, it was about me letting go.

I will never forget that phone call. When I told her what God wanted me to do and how painful and frightened I was, I cried and she cried. We both confessed our insecurities to one another which oddly comforted and encouraged us. It was one of the hardest things the Lord had asked me to do at that point in my life.

This was to begin a long journey of identity transformation and liberation. In some ways those days seem so long ago, and yet in other ways they are exactly the same now as then. I have found the scenery and circumstances change with each level of identity reshaping, but the methods that God has used in my life remain the same.

> *Do not remember the former things, nor*
> *consider the things of old.*
> *Behold, I will do a new thing, now it shall*
> *spring forth; shall you not know it?*
> *I will even make a road in the wilderness*
> *and rivers in the desert.*
> Isaiah 43:18-19

Chapter 2

The Battle Belongs
To the Lord

Even after serving the Lord and witnessing Him use me, I still had a lot of hang ups. I could not stand in front of people. I still had feelings of inferiority, insecurity, and intimidation, especially after stepping down from the women's ministry. I felt like I was lost and drifting aimlessly. What was I to do? I thought I had to live with all of it. Yet to live with it seemed to hinder me. It seemed to be like a weight that kept me down so that I could not lift off the ground. I honestly did not know what to do.

It was difficult to have this inward calling wanting to take off and fly and yet have this outward weight keeping me down. I would like to tell you the answers came right away but it would actually take years.

An image of being a failure had been built on the inside of me and it was hindering me.

While serving under the leadership of my pastor, I was trying to fly but it seemed I was always hitting the ceiling. I tried so hard to be a blessing. People did not seem to accept me. My pastor would tell me later, many of those around me were jealous of me. I did not get it. Didn't they know my past? Did they not know where I had come from? Did they not know how hard it was for me? Thoughts of not answering the call were always on my mind. At times I would weep and beg God to leave me alone. But "it" was always there. "It" was God's divine appointment for me.

The Call

One day I would pray, "Use me Lord" and the next day I would pray, "Please take 'it' away." I was caught between a heart that loved God and wanted to please Him and a consciousness of my bad choices.

There is something very powerful about the call of God upon a life; it is a driving force that won't quit. It maneuvers you to go places you may not want to go. It beckons you to pursue when you may want to give up. When I try to define the call of God, I tell people I love God and He has asked me to do something about the love I have for Him. My love for Him won't let me abandon the call He has placed on my life.

If being chased by the call were not enough, there were people who did not approve of my being in the ministry. Something had to be done and something had to get settled. First of all, the Lord showed me a verse from the Bible.

> *For the gifts and the calling of God*
> *are irrevocable.*
>
> (Romans 11:29)

He had called me and I began to realize this war was not just going to go away. It was going to have to be fought and won! But how do I fight yet alone win? Victory would come by having to fight many battles.

Battles to Fight

Prior to meeting my pastor and settling in his church, my family and I were attending a local Pentecostal church. When the pastor told us he was leaving and wanted us to follow, we went without any questions. This would prove to be a great test. I would like to say this is not about the people involved, but about what God wanted to do in me.

After several months, I sat down with the pastor and shared the vision I had when I was ten years old. I expressed my desire for a mentor. I was not prepared for what was to come. He told me that until God spoke to him about a call on my life, he would not believe it or encourage it. Further more, he perceived me to be an outspoken woman who needed to go home and find her place. I was devastated, hurt and angry. I was angry at this man and at God. I had tried and failed again. I wanted to run but God would not let me.

Rather than getting a chance to learn how to fly, my wings seem clipped. Behind the scenes, God was doing something in me. He was teaching me to know His voice and His will.

To make a very long year short, this man became involved with false doctrine and through the safety of godly counsel and revelation from the Word; I was released to go forward. I carried with me a new confidence and a renewed strength.

Another battle was soon to follow. A woman minister came to hold a revival meeting in Pastor John's church. The Lord used her powerfully. At the close of the meeting, I asked her to pray for me. I shared with her how I could feel the anointing come on me but I could not seem to get it to flow from me.

She asked me what I thought my calling was and I replied by saying, "An evangelist." She told me that was my first mistake, that I was frustrating the grace of God by trying to step outside my calling of a teacher to be an evangelist. I was crushed and again I felt like a loser. I also felt like I had missed hearing the voice of God (a battle I just thought I had won).

As I was driving home that night, I again wanted to quit. I was devastated, hurt and angry. Instead of quitting, I had a talk with Jesus. He told me to read 1 Kings 13. I read it but it didn't make much sense to me. So I read it again . . . And again. I still wasn't getting it. I prayed and asked the Lord to show me what He wanted me to see. The words from verses 15 through 18 began to minister to me personally.

> *Then he said to him, "Come home*
> *with me and eat bread." And he said,*
> *"I cannot return with you nor go in*
> *with you; neither can I eat bread nor*
> *drink water with you in this place.*
> *For I have been told by the word of*
> *the Lord, 'You shall not eat bread*
> *nor drink water there, nor return by*
> *going the way you came.'" He said to*
> *him, "I too am a prophet as you are,*
> *and an angel spoke to me by the word*
> *of the Lord, saying, 'Bring him back*
> *with you to your house, that he may*
> *eat bread and drink water.'" (He was*
> *lying to him.)*

God was saying that the young prophet had heard a true word. He had very specific instructions from the Lord Himself. The older prophet was speaking a lie. I was seeing this woman as a seasoned minister who had to know more than me. I doubted my own ability to hear from the Lord just as the younger prophet doubted his. It was as if the Lord was saying, "Your life and ministry depend on obedience to My words." I was representing the younger prophet!

> *And he cried out to the man of God*
> *who came from Judah, saying, "Thus*
> *says the Lord: 'Because you have*

> *disobeyed the word of the Lord, and*
> *have not kept the commandment which*
> *the Lord your God commanded you,*
> *but you came back, ate bread, and*
> *drank water in the place of which the*
> *Lord said to you, "Eat no bread and*
> *drink no water," your corpse shall not*
> *come to the tomb of your fathers."'*
>
> (1 Kings 13:21-22)

The Lord was making it clear to me that if I didn't heed Him, it could cost me my life and forfeit my ministry. I have never forgotten that lesson. It was a tremendous victory.

The Battle of Intimidation

During this time, I had met an evangelist from Oklahoma whom I recognized as a divine appointment. This man came across sure, confident, and bold. I possessed none of those qualities and found myself intimidated. He saw something in me and was doing his best to help. I had prayed for and desperately wanted help, but I was unable to accept it.

Year after year, he would come back into our community, and time and time again, he would speak to my life by the Holy Spirit. Over the years, he even began to give me opportunities to minister, for which I was grateful but still insecure. I felt like I didn't "measure up." I had a failure mentality and I had to get free.

A time came when our families were going on a mission trip together but just before we were to leave, intimidation arrested me. I had tremendous doubts and fears. I labored in prayer all night asking God to help me discover the source of all this fear.

Through the victory of prayer, the Lord showed me my inferior mind-set. I saw this man standing tall like a stately oak tree and I saw myself as a grasshopper.

The Lord had a solution and He led me to Numbers 13:27, 28. God had just sent out the spies into Canaan. Ten came back with a bad report, but Caleb, who had a "different spirit" . . . a spirit of faith, came back with a good report. Those with the bad report saw the blessings of God, but because of the size of the enemy, they were paralyzed and doubtful. God had just been dwarfed in their eyes and had become unable.

> *. . . It truly flows with milk and honey, and this is its fruit. Nevertheless the people who dwell in the land are strong; the cities are fortified and very large; moreover we saw the descendants of Anak there.*

They were willing to say, "God this land is good, your promise was true, but. . ." The problem wasn't with God and the problem wasn't with the enemy, it was with them.

> *But the men who had gone up with him said, "We are not able to go up against the people, for they are stronger than we." And they gave the children of Israel a bad report of the land which they had spied out, saying, "The land through which we have gone as spies is a land that devours its inhabitants, and all the people whom we saw in it are men of great stature. There we saw the giants (the descendants of Anak came from the giants); and we were like grasshoppers in our own sight, and so we were in their sight."*
>
> (Numbers 13:31-33)

How you see yourself is how the enemy sees you. Intimidation always directs your eyes to the wrong thing. The problem was the ten spies were not able to break out of the mind-set of intimidation. Fear will paralyze you. This one thing I know, fear will keep you walking the perimeter of your Promise Land rather than letting you enter in.

Prior to leaving on this mission trip, I had discovered that I was terrified of this evangelist getting to know me. I was convinced that if he got to know the "real me," he would no longer offer ministry opportunities to me.

I have found a secret, there is a risk in being known, but unless we are willing to risk being known, we will not walk free from fear and intimidation.

The next morning I had an appointment to meet with this man and his wife. The Holy Spirit had spoken to me that night in prayer and told me I had to tell this man how I felt. I had to face my giant and I could not run. The Lord might as well have said to take a bullet in the heart. What He was asking was that difficult for me because I highly respected this minister.

I was caught between a heart that loved God and wanted to please Him and a self-consciousness of intimidation. I knew I had to obey the Lord, but this was by far one of the hardest things I had ever done.

The Lord doesn't always remove the mountains we face but sometimes requires us to climb them. The good news is that He is always right there along side us.

> *Let your conduct be without covetousness; be content with such things as you have. For He Himself has said, "I will never leave you nor forsake you." So we may boldly say: "The Lord is my helper, I will not fear. What can man do to me?"'*
>
> (Hebrews 13:5-6)

I was very nervous and distracted the next morning but finally mustered up enough courage to tell the evangelist I had something I needed to say to him. He said, "So say it." I blurted out, "You intimidate me." There I said it. "No one can intimidate you unless you let them," he said. He had quoted 1 Peter

5:7 so many times, *"Casting your care upon Him, for He cares for you."* This time I listened. I finally understood.

Something literally changed. God's power had really set me free from the opinions of men. It was easy to give it to the Lord. For the first time I was beginning to see that God wanted me to see myself as an equal.

The Battle of Insecurity

I used to stutter over the word prr. . .prr. . .pree. . .ach even though I knew the call of God was on my life. When I could get it out, it wasn't very loud or sure.

Although doors were opening, I still felt insecure and remained crippled by a lack of confidence. I was not sure anyone wanted or needed anything I had to offer. Honestly I was convinced it wasn't much.

Whining about it one day, the Holy Spirit spoke to me, "I AM!" "Yeah, Lord, I know," I flippantly replied. "No you don't," I heard Him say back to me. Have you ever noticed how the Holy Spirit seems to be able to get your attention? "Okay Lord what do you mean?" I asked. He said it again, "I AM."

He began to show me that like Moses, my insecurity stemmed from a wrong focus. I was so busy looking at *my* insecurities, that I could not see *His* ability. He was saying, "You may have made some mistakes and experienced some failure, but you must get your eyes off you and place your focus upon Me."

I silently thought to myself, "I *am* just a house-wife from Indiana. I *am* a high school drop out. I *am* now a mother of two children without any Bible training. I *am* a teen-age pregnant statistic. . ." In the middle of all this, the Lord bursts into my thoughts declaring, "I AM that I am!"

He was saying, "You are too self-conscious. Now stop it! If you will keep your eyes fixed on Me, I will use you. Place your confidence in Me. See that I am the greater One and I live in *you*!" If you are going to do anything great for God, you will also have to come to this place of revelation. (We will discuss how to lose self-consciousness in chapter four).

Like Moses, I was limiting God because my eyes were focused on me and the things I had done or on things I didn't have. God did not accept Moses' excuses and He wasn't accepting mine. He will not accept yours either. There is good news. God didn't give up on Moses. He didn't give up on me. He won't give up on you. Thankfully, He is very patient.

I have experienced and witnessed how insecurity hinders God's people. Insecurities result from an unhealthy focus of the past. Insecurity tried to hinder Paul, too, but he had to get victory just the like the rest of us.

> *Brethren, I do not count myself to have apprehended; but one thing I do, forgetting those things which are behind and reaching forward to those things which are ahead, I press toward the goal for the prize of the upward*

> *call of God in Christ Jesus. Therefore*
> *let us, as many as are mature, have*
> *this mind; and if in anything you think*
> *otherwise, God will reveal even this*
> *to you.*

(Philippians 3:13-15)

Paul recognized where he was but he also saw that the God who called him offered him a greater future. He was willing to let go of the past to embrace his future. We have to do that too. The Lord spoke this truth to me, "It is very difficult to walk forward always looking backward."

Paul also made a choice to *forget* the things that were behind him. I have found one thing to be true: It is a waste of time to "rewind" the past because you cannot erase it, but you can let it go. Paul could stand still or move forward. He chose to go forward and indicated that it is a continual choice and on-going process. With the prize of eternal life in sight, Paul's focus turned from the past to his future completion. It was full speed ahead and Paul had a new focus. When we can turn our focus from ourselves and our past, we gain renewed vision seeing that Jesus Himself is our reward! This gives us ability and desire to finish the race. And the race can only be finished and won as we keep our eyes on the prize!

The Lord helped me to see that it was my choice: I could look at me or I could look at Him. I could have my insecurity or His ability. Revelation comes, and when we mix faith with it, it becomes ours. We can then move forward: No longer victims but as victors.

> *You are of God little children, and have overcome them, because He who is in you is greater than he who is in the world.*
>
> (1 John 4:4)

The Necessity of Vision

I would like to say one thing here about vision: "*Where there is no revelation, the people cast off restraint . . .*" (Proverbs 29:18).

A gymnast who trains six days a week for eight hours a day has a vision. She has a revelation; "I have what it takes to be a champion." The gold medal is her prize and everyday she keeps that prize before her. It is her strength when she is tired. It is her push when she wants to stop. It is her fight when she wants to quit.

In Philippians chapter three, Paul was saying that he kept the heavenly invitation before him constantly. It propelled him forward. It brought him strength and endurance. It brought discipline as well. Paul did not want to be disqualified (see 1 Corinthians 9:27) so he ran well and he ran fair.

The gymnast refrains from binging on pizza, cupcakes, and milkshakes, because she wants to be an Olympic gold medalist. In the same way, when you and I receive revelatory vision, or a word from the Lord, we must refrain from things that hinder us from pursuing our objective.

For the gymnast, the medal becomes more important than the milkshakes. She is unwilling to exchange her goal and dream for a temporary lapse or craving. She is not willing to settle for a short term fix, but is willing to patiently wait for her life long dream.

Every one needs a vision.

The Battle of Inferiority

Although I had begun to realize that God wanted me to see myself as a minister, an equal with others, I had not completely mastered that hurdle. God began to help me realize He had "fearfully and wonderfully made me" (Psalm 139). He was constantly showing me that He had placed me in the body of Christ as He saw fit. It was His right to use me as He wanted. I didn't have the right to refuse.

> *But indeed, O man, who are you to reply against God? Will the thing formed say to him who formed it, "Why have you made me like this?" Does not the potter have power over the clay, from the same lump to make one vessel for honor and another for dishonor?*

(Romans 9:20-21)

48

It became more and more clear that I was not my own. The Lord graciously reminded me that He had bought me with the price of His life.

What about the "woman question?" I had been taught that women were not allowed to be ministers. Women could be Sunday school teachers and missionaries, but not preachers. I was female but this "male" desire was like fire shut up in my bones. I often wondered if God had made a mistake. My identity was in a serious crisis. I did not know who I was according to the Word of God. Instead, my identity had been formed by the opinions and teachings of man.

Time and time again I would seek God for answers. I read books about the "woman question" but I only read the ones written by male authors just to be safe. Men seemed to come out of the wood work to tell me what they thought about my ambitions. It was so difficult. God began to show me the battle did not belong to me but to Him. He was asking me the question, "Will you let Me fight your battles?" With God for me, who could be against me, right?

I began to see through the Word of God that I had to make up my mind to either please men or please God. I brought all of my excuses before the Lord. I had revelation that one day I will give an account to God for all of my actions. He is the greater one to fear. Knowing that I will have to give an account to Him makes me weigh every decision very carefully and seek Him humbly in prayer. I fear the Lord more than man so I do my best to be sure that I am hearing accurately from Him.

The Lord took me to the story of Bartimaeus (Mark 10:46-52) and I realized that Bartimaeus would still be blind had he *listened* to the opinions of people. He was blind and wanted to see. I have to imagine that as he sat by the gate daily, he heard the many reports of Jesus. When he heard that Jesus was coming his way, he cried out *"Son of David, have mercy on me!"* The crowd told him to be quiet but he would not listen! He wanted something from the Master and he was unwilling to let the opportunity pass him by. He was desperate to see. Jesus heard his plea and called for him. Those same people who had just told him to be quiet were now relaying Jesus' response. Those who were once against him were now for him because Jesus was.

Overcoming many hurdles and watching the Lord fight many battles for me, I have since become surrounded by many, including men, who sanction, approve, and honor me.

I will forever be grateful to the Lord who has approved my ministry because to be called in the ministry is the highest calling and privilege. I take it very seriously.

> *Now He who establishes us with you in Christ and has anointed us is God, who has also sealed us and given us the Spirit in our hearts as a guarantee.*
>
> (2 Corinthians 1:21-22)

And we have such trust through Christ toward God. Not that we are sufficient of ourselves to think of anything as being from ourselves, but our sufficiency is from God, who also made us sufficient as ministers of the new covenant, not of the letter but of the Spirit; for the letter kills, but the Spirit gives life.

(2 Corinthians 3:4-6)

Then God said, "Let Us make man in Our image, according to Our likeness...
So God created man in His own image; in the image of God He created him; male and female He created them.
Genesis 1:26, 27

Chapter 3

The Problem with Self Consciousness

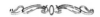

Several great battles had been fought and won, thank God! However, I was still finding some difficulty walking in the anointing of the Holy Spirit. My greatest desire and the prayer I probably prayed more than any other went like this: "Lord I want the anointing. I want to see heart-felt conviction fall on the lost. I want to see the deaf hear, the dumb speak, and the blind see. I want to see captives set free. I want an anointing that will affect cancer. Lord, please anoint me to preach."

The desire was there, the prayers had been prayed and the call had been confirmed. I saw some results but not to the degree I wanted and I struggled with that. God wanted me to lay hands on the sick but I questioned whether I had enough "stuff." I wanted the Holy Spirit to flow through me to be a blessing to others. I wanted to be used by Him. I wanted to walk in the anointing, the kind that destroys yokes of sickness and bondage, but I was a little scared to step out.

Prophecies had been given to me confirming the gift of healing and the call of God to preach. I had been specific in my prayers for confirmation about these matters. The earliest word came in April, 1984. A husband and wife team from Texas had come to our area and spoke this word to me through the gift of the Holy Spirit.

> *For there's even a new mantle and a fresh mantle of anointing on you and you're gonna feel more responsibility. You're gonna feel more "conscious" of even your call and the gift that God has put in you. There's a real substance that's gonna flow from you. I can just see it flowing forth out of your arms and fingers. And you're not to hesitate; you're not to be shy about laying hands on people with needs because there are needs that are going to be met. There's a healing flow that's gonna flow forth from you.*

Who me? How? When? What if nothing happens? What if people don't get healed? What if I make a fool of myself? I did not know how to get over this hurdle, but I wanted to so bad!

With my eyes wide open, I watched everyone who had an anointing. I observed to learn everything

I could. They made it look so easy. I knew it had something to do with faith, something to do with being called, and something to do with obedience. But how do I get there?

A few years later, on July 14, 1988, the evangelist from Oklahoma gave me this word.

>*If you look at what you've got, it's already good. God would say to you, "Stand still!" He knows you want to get out there and get with it. He knows! He knows! And the door will open; the time will be to go. When it's right the answer shall be bright and you'll walk in total daylight. As of yet, you are a little scared to thrust out there. You are moved about by upheaval and care, but you shall walk by the gift of faith. This is your greatest desire to climb up higher. Your heart is precious in my sight, I want you to know. Your anointing is increasing as you go. So stand still; see the salvation of the Lord! Move as I move and we'll move together as one. Yes! Yes! Yes! A ministry like the manner of Kathryn Kuhlman you desire and you shall be set, set on fire. Oh my daughter hours to weep and to lay at My face, now is the time to enter the race. Oh stay small in your own eyes as I begin to use thee because the power of God*

> *shall effectively flow. Others will be jealous of the anointing. Know that I am your source and I will direct your course.*

"Are you sure you have the right person?" was my thought. Even though I did want this to be true I could not see myself doing it. These words were my prayers. These people could not possibly know all that had been in my heart, but God did. And He was letting me know it.

The next several years would be a great time of growing for me. I continued to seek the Lord for fulfillment of all that was in my heart and all that had been spoken.

During this time, the Lord began to speak to me about promotion. He was directing me to move from teaching the Word to preaching. I told Him I did not know how. Thank God the Holy Spirit is a teacher. Another minister and friend began speaking to me about recognizing the call of God on my life. He would later ordain me in the early part of 1993.

Immediately after this, I felt as if the Lord told me to get an education. For me, I knew the credentials would be the difference in people taking me seriously. From that time on, I began to go to Bible College through correspondence courses. I was certified to minister in March of 1994, and licensed to preach in 1995 with the Assemblies of God.

Before I stepped out there, I asked the Lord for a confirmation. I was very specific about the word "preach" but I told no one about it.

On June 5, 1995, this word came forth from the Holy Spirit through an evangelist.

> *Sister, will you come? I saw a vision of you and I need to speak to you prophetically. You see, according to the Bible, in Acts chapter two, Peter said, "My sons and daughters shall prophesy. . . I will show signs and wonders."*

> *I see you holding a Bible standing, speaking and tears fill your eyes because you're a female. They also come against you. Ministry has come against you because they're intimidated and they're jealous, but what you must do is maintain a sweet, humble spirit and God will exalt you even further with or without their help, with or without their approval.*

> *Know that the seal of God is upon you. He has called you and placed within you the gift to "preach" His gospel! Be not afraid to speak, my daughter, for I have called you and ordained you from the foundation of the world. The gift in you is not man made. I have placed it in there.*

Hallelujah! God said it! It wasn't just me. It was His calling and not just my idea. God is so good! He meets us where we are. The Lord was letting me know He recognized my struggles. He understood the hardships. More importantly, He knew my heart!

The Problem Defined

I would like to tell you that this word from the Lord fixed everything. The question, "Am I called or not called to preach?" had finally been answered and confirmed. Having it settled was an enormous victory. What about the anointing, the ability and the power of God?

Not long after this, a great revelation was given to me that would change my life, a revelation that would release my ministry into a greater dimension. I am excited to share it with you, and really, this is why I am writing this book. The Lord led me to Genesis.

> *And they were both naked, the man*
> *and his wife, and were not ashamed.*
> (Genesis 2:25)

Logic says they were comfortable because they only *knew* what was right. There were no evil thoughts to deal with. This is true, but it seemed the Lord was also saying something more to me.

> *Now the serpent was more cunning*
> *than any beast of the field which the*

Lord God had made. And he said to the woman, "Has God indeed said, 'You shall not eat of every tree of the garden?'" And the woman said to the serpent, "We may eat the fruit of the trees of the garden; but of the fruit of the tree which is in the midst of the garden, God has said, 'You shall not eat of it, nor shall you touch it lest you die.'"

Then the serpent said to the woman, "You shall not surely die. For God knows that in the day you eat of it your eyes will be opened, and you will be like God, knowing good and evil."

So when the woman saw that the tree was good for food, that it was pleasant to the eyes, and a tree desirable to make one wise, she took of its fruit and ate. She also gave to her husband with her, and he ate.

Then the eyes of both of them were opened, and they knew that they were naked; and they sewed fig leaves together and made themselves coverings.

And they heard the sound of the Lord God walking in the garden in the cool

*of the day, and Adam and his wife
hid themselves from the presence of
the Lord God among the trees of the
garden. Then the Lord God called to
Adam and said to him, "Where are
you?" So he said, "I heard Your voice
in the garden, and I was afraid because
I was naked; and I hid myself."*

*And He said, "Who told you that you
were naked? Have you eaten from the
tree of which I commanded you that
you should not eat." Then the man
said, "The woman whom You gave to
be with me, she gave me of the tree,
and I ate." And the Lord God said to
the woman, "What is this you have
done?" The woman said, "The serpent
deceived me, and I ate."*

(Genesis 3:1-13)

The Lord showed me that verse six changed
the whole world. I understand that Adam and Eve
disobeyed God. I am not trying to take away from
that truth. We know that after the serpent spoke with
Eve, the tree looked good. I do not think she even
considered the tree before that time, but now, all of
a sudden, it looked really good. It became desirable.
Eve had her heart and mind set on something other
than God because her eyes were opened!

Through disobedience sin entered into the world,
and what was once natural and comfortable (naked-

ness) was now shameful. This couple was married so nudity wasn't the issue. Sex wasn't the issue. Perhaps it was the thoughts that came in discovering that they were naked. I am sure the enemy was flooding their minds with accusations (Revelation 12:10).

Therefore, self-consciousness had now entered their lives. Thoughts for other things were now a part of their focus. Before this, they enjoyed walks and conversation with the Lord (verse eight). Now shameful, they felt the need to run from God's presence and hide. Not only did they want to hide, they wanted to be covered. Fear has now entered the scene of their relationship with God (v.10).

The serpent appealed to Eve's pride by suggesting that God had an ulterior motive in commanding them not to eat of the tree of the knowledge of good and evil (The Nelson Study Bible, p. 9). It raised the question, "What is it that God doesn't want me to know?" The Lord was not against Adam and Eve having knowledge. He wanted them to learn, but in relationship to Himself. When this doubt entered the picture, the focus turned from God to looking out for self.

Adam and Eve had once enjoyed perfect fellowship with the Lord but now they were distracted and running from Him. This all started to sound very familiar to me. I could see this had been a problem in my own life. I was distracted by the memories of my past. I was running from the call of God due to shame and humiliation. Fear and intimidation had been uncovering me and leaving me helpless and cowering. I was being hindered from an intimate relationship with Him due to self-consciousness.

Now God was showing me that it was time to take back what the enemy had stolen . . . my born-again identity!

> *That you put off, concerning your former*
> *conduct, the old man which grows corrupt*
> *according to the deceitful lusts, and be*
> *renewed in the spirit of your mind, and that*
> *you put on the new man which was*
> *created according to God, in true*
> *righteousness and holiness.*
> Ephesians 4:22-24

Chapter 4

Losing Self-Consciousness

W hen we are born-again, we become a new creation. The old is gone and the new comes (2 Corinthians 5:17). This means the slate is wiped clean. Our sins are erased and we are given a brand new beginning; a new life without any mistakes in it. If you are like me, it didn't take long after being born-again to make some new mistakes. Thank God for I John 1:9, *"If we confess our sins, He is faithful and just to forgive us our sins and to cleanse us from all unrighteousness."* This verse allows our slate to remain clean. I call this verse the eraser of the Bible.

Now that God had shown me it was up to me to reclaim my born-again identity, I had to ask Him how to do that. He began to speak to me in very elementary terms. He told me I had to lose self-consciousness; that thing that kept speaking all the "what if I" questions and the "I am just . . ." statements. I had to return to God-consciousness because it is the only way to live a productive life.

My youngest daughter, Kendra, brought back to life the revelation of living a life of self-consciousness. When she would do something wrong, like take cookies without asking, she would run for our glass coffee table and hide. I would question her in much the same way the Lord God questioned Adam. "What are you doing, Kendra?" "Nothing mother," would come her reply. Her wrong doing uncovered her and caused her to hide. I had to laugh because she didn't realize I could see her. In her mind, she *thought* she was hidden from me. The Lord spoke to me and said, "My people are much like that." Adam and Eve were like that. I was like that, but nothing is hidden from the Lord.

Like my daughter, I still needed to renew the way I thought. God did not want me to continue to live my life with a failure mentality. He did not want me to continue to reproduce intimidation and fear.

The Truth Will Set You Free

Losing self-consciousness requires renewing your mind.

To be "covered" and secure again Kendra needed to admit she had done something wrong. I might have to discipline her (depending on her wrong action), but afterward I would explain to her why she was in trouble. Then, I could comfort her. In the same way, Adam and Eve had to admit to the *truth*, "We ate." God's response was not silence. It was not yelling and screaming. It was not even immediate death. It was a conversation; a calm, loving, merciful conversation filled with questions to help locate Adam and Eve for their own sake (Genesis 3:11).

They tried to fix themselves. They tried to cover themselves. "... *They sewed fig leaves together and made themselves coverings*" (Genesis 3:7). I too tried to fix myself. I tried to cover up and bury my insecurity and failure mentality. I tried to *will* myself to change, but every attempt failed. Adam and Eve's attempts didn't work either.

Animals had to die in order for Adam and Eve to be covered and Jesus died so that you and I might be covered and have newness of life. As the New Testament states, "... *and without shedding of blood there is no remission*" (Hebrews 9:22). Jesus' death provided a way of escape from sin which caused a destructive self-conscious mind-set! The Lord did not leave them where they were! "*Also for Adam and his wife the Lord God made tunics of skin, and clothed them*" (Genesis 3:21). His mercy reached past their disobedience.

Yes, there were consequences. Things would now become hard. Life would know labor and work. Physical death was the result, but thanks be to God, though we die physically, yet shall we live and never die (John 11:25-26). Jesus is our resurrection and life! This is the good news, not only will He one day raise us up together to meet Him in the air, but He lifts us up here and now. I know He has done it for me time and time again.

Elementary Principles

Losing self-consciousness results when we know and believe the truth.

Wow, what an eye opening revelation for me! "What do you want me to do with it all, Lord?" He told me to take the truth, His Word (His conversation with us) and renew my mind. I found ten scriptures and began to put truth where fear and failure had once dominated. I wrote them on index cards and read them daily.

You have to remember I was questioning God, "Do *I* have enough stuff?" I was seeking the anointing. I wanted to have a walk worthy of the calling on my life. I wanted to go higher, to a new level. I wanted to see the supernatural, and I wanted God to use me.

These are *my* ten scriptures:

> *And I thank Christ Jesus our Lord who has enabled me, because He counted me faithful, putting me into the ministry.*
>
> (1 Timothy 1:12)

> *Now He who establishes us with you in Christ and has anointed us is God, who also has sealed us and given us the Spirit in our hearts as a guarantee.*
>
> (2 Corinthians 1:21-22)

And we have such trust through Christ toward God. Not that we are sufficient of ourselves to think of anything as being from ourselves, but our sufficiency is from God, who also made us sufficient ministers of the new covenant, not of the letter but of the Spirit; for the letter kills, but the Spirit gives life.

(2 Corinthians 3:4-6)

And He said to them, "Go into all the world and preach the gospel to every creature. And these signs will follow those who believe: In My name they will cast out demons; they will speak with new tongues; they will take up serpents; and if they drink anything deadly, it will by no means hurt them; they will lay hands on the sick, and they will recover."

(Mark 16:15, 17-18)

And they went out and preached everywhere, the Lord working with them and confirming the word through the accompanying signs. Amen.

(Mark 16:20)

This charge I commit to you, son Timothy, according to the prophecies previously made concerning you, that by them you may wage the good warfare.

(1Timothy 1:18)

He who calls you is faithful, who also will do it.

(1 Thessalonians 5:24)

Therefore I remind you to stir up the gift of God which is in you through the laying on of my hands. For God has not given us a spirit of fear, but of power and of love and of a sound mind.

(2 Timothy 1:6-7)

For in Him dwells all the fullness of the Godhead bodily; and you are complete in Him, who is the head of all principality and power.

(Colossians 2:9-10)

Do not neglect the gift that is in you, which was given to you by prophecy with the laying on of the hands of the eldership. Meditate of these things; give yourself entirely to them, that your progress may be evident to all.

(1Timothy 4:14-15)

The writer of Hebrews tells us that the Word of God is alive and powerful. I can testify to the truthfulness of that statement. As I began to hide God's Word in my heart, it began to change my mind, my thoughts, and my mentality. Where I had once seen myself unable, I could see Jesus not only able, but willing. Where I had once seen only me, I now could at last see that He was bigger and greater. It was all about Jesus living in me not *me* trying to live for Jesus. The truth will cause you to see freedom, know freedom, and experience freedom. This elementary revelation from God changed my life and renewed my mind.

Free From Distraction

Losing self-consciousness will result when we feel covered and secure.

Through the revelation of Genesis three, I could see the devil's ploy was to get man's eyes off the Lord and on himself. He knew if he could achieve this feat, man would be powerless. That was where I was living and I did not like it.

When I began to see that the enemy used Eve to get her eyes off the Lord, I could see my own life. The enemy loves to use distraction. Satan is an expert in using our fleshly desires against us. He counts on our appetites distracting us from the Lord.

> *For those who live according to the flesh set their minds on the things of the flesh, but those who live according to the Spirit, the things of the Spirit. For to be carnally minded is death,*

> *but to be spiritually minded is life and*
> *peace.*
>
> (Romans 8:5-6)

A better way of saying this is, "Those, whose minds are occupied with distractions of fleshly, physical or natural things, will know and experience death." This was true of Adam and Eve. They were distracted from the Lord through a natural thing, a tree, but a *forbidden* tree. They couldn't be content with *all* the other trees because the enemy appealed to their carnal appetite. We need to understand this strategy of the enemy in order to conquer him.

I, too, was distracted from the Lord through my carnal (unregenerate), natural, and fleshly thoughts. Not only was I distracted from Him, but also away from His plans and purposes.

Distractions Purposes

1. Distraction is used to render us powerless. Jesus said, ". . . *for without Me you can do nothing*" (John 15:5). There is a whole lot of "nothing" going on because it is being done without Jesus. "Nothing" is the only thing that can be produced by self.

2. Distraction is used to hinder us from bearing fruit. Jesus said, "*Abide in Me, and I in you. As the branch cannot bear fruit of itself, unless it abides in the vine, neither can you, unless you abide in Me*" (John 15:4). The devil has always been

after God's glory. When we do not bear fruit, the Father is not glorified. When we do not bear fruit, we fail to be His disciples (John 15:8). We must make a conscious decision to depend on Jesus to be fruitful.

3. Distraction is used to sever our relationship. Jesus said, "*If anyone does not abide in Me, he is cast out as a branch. . .*" (John 15:6). The enemy wants to get you following something other than the Lord so that he can erode your relationship. If he can not get you following something else, he will try to get you to follow people. He will use anything or anyone he can to get you to move away from your intimacy with Jesus. Remember Jesus said, ". . . *without* (apart from or severed from) *Me you can do nothing*" (John 15:5).

4. Distraction is used so that we will grow weary. Jesus states, ". . . *and is withered. . .*" (John 15:6). Distraction takes our energy, effort, and efficiency. Because distraction comes through the appetites, it usually produces sin. James said, "*But each one is tempted when he is drawn away by his own desires and enticed. Then, when desire has conceived, it gives birth to sin; and sin, when it is full-grown, brings forth death*" (James 1:14-15). It is interesting how much energy we have to do what we want, but very little when it comes to doing what God wants us to do.

5. Distraction is used to bring loss. Jesus said, ". . . *and they are burned*" (John 15:6). Some commentator's say this refers to judgment; indicating a loss of reward. With this being true, Paul said, we are to take heed how we build (works) on the foundation, which is Christ. How we build and with what we build will become evident. If the work, endures, there will be a reward. If the work is burned, the person will suffer loss (1 Corinthians 3:10-15). I want something to take to the Father, don't you?

6. Distraction affects our prayers. "*If you abide in Me, and My words abide in you, you will ask what you desire, and it shall be done for you*" (John 15:7). There is a condition with the word "if." The Word of God ignites the right desires. The right desires formulate the right prayers. The right prayers will be answered (James 4:3). Distracted prayers usually are selfish in nature and are not answered.

Freedom from distraction comes when our minds are occupied with spiritual, supernatural, and heavenly thoughts. Paul told the saints at Rome that to be occupied with spiritual things was life and peace (Romans 8:6). Who doesn't want life and peace?

> *Set your mind on things that are*
> *above, not on things on the earth.*
>   (Colossians 3:2)

Do you want to know what occupies your life? Do you want to know if it is fleshly or spiritual? You have to examine your thought life. Believe me, it will tell you where you are. The good thing is once you locate where you are, you can make the necessary adjustments to move from your present location.

Peace to Pray

Losing self-consciousness results when we are at peace.

Paul, writing from prison, encouraged the church at Philippi to rejoice. He wasn't satisfied saying it once; he had to say it twice. He then went on to exhort them not to be anxious about anything. He explains that this is possible by committing everything to the Lord in prayer and having a thankful heart. Prayer is the answer for every occasion! He promises there will be peace; peace that guards not only the heart but the mind as well (Philippians 4:4, 6-7).

This type of prayer moves the mind from the natural (fleshly) to focus on the Lord who is able and willing. It moves the mind to focus on the truth of God's Word. Peace in the heart brings peace to the mind.

> *Finally, brethren, whatever things are*
> *true, whatever things are noble, what-*

> *ever things are just, whatever things*
> *are pure, whatever things are lovely,*
> *whatever things are of good report,*
> *if there is any virtue and if there is*
> *anything praiseworthy. . . meditate on*
> *these things.*
>
> (Philippians 4:8)

Peace in the mind brings peace to our lives. A life at peace is exhibiting trust in the Lord, a right focus, and a consciousness of God.

> *Trust (lean on, rely on, and be confi-*
> *dent) in the Lord and do good; so*
> *shall you dwell in the land and feed*
> *surely on His faithfulness, and truly*
> *you shall be fed. Delight yourself also*
> *in the Lord, and He will give you the*
> *desires and secret petitions of your*
> *heart.*
>
> (Psalm 37:3-4, Amplified)

The mind that *feeds* on His faithfulness, rather than its self, is healthy. Then he is able to delight himself in the Lord. He is able to think on what God wants. Then he will have the desires of God's heart spring up in him, and those desires will not be refused.

Secret prayers and petitions of the heart are precious to the Lord, and He delights in giving them to His children. This reminds me of Jesus' words in Matthew 6:33, "*But seek first the kingdom of God and His righteousness, and all these things shall be added unto you."*

When we seek to live in right standing with the Lord, He withholds nothing from us. When we keep our focus and attention on Him, He takes care of everything. Most of our thoughts and prayers reflect our need, they reveal that we are concerned about the things we put on and the things we eat (Matthew 6:25-32). The Bible calls this worry, and Jesus tells us not to worry. He is declaring He is trustworthy!

What we feed on is what we will see.

Now faith is the substance of things hoped for,
the evidence of things not seen.
Hebrews 11:1

Chapter 5

Rebuilding the Right Image

There is an old saying, "You are what you eat." If this is to be true of natural things, why would it not be true of spiritual things? We are to feed on the Lord's faithfulness so if we feed or graze on the Word, we will be fed, nourished, and tended to. If we trust in the Lord, we will have our needs met.

In Exodus 34, Moses met the Lord on Mount Sinai and he received the Ten Commandments. He spent forty days and nights with God. After being in God's presence and talking with Him (verse 29), Moses' face was aglow with the glory of the Lord! Looking at God *transformed* Moses' appearance. In the same way, looking into the perfect law of liberty, the Bible transforms our perception of how we see things.

Paul wrote the church at Corinth (2 Corinthians 3) testifying that the glory of the New Covenant was greater than the old. He explained how a veil of spiritual blindness sits on the minds of the Israelites because they rejected Jesus. Their inward perception could not conceive that a carpenter, son of Mary and Joseph, was the Messiah.

This word *"minds"* (2 Corinthians 3:14) in the Greek explains this to be a perception of the intellect or thoughts. It denotes thoughts, which are thought out (The New Strong's Expanded Exhaustive Concordance, p. 172). As they thought about the possibility of Jesus being the Messiah, and because they could not conceive it, their actions acted out their thoughts. Those actions were rejection of Him. It was the result of rational reflection on an inward perception of thoughts. We could say then we live out what we think about.

The veil or blindness is removed the moment we "see" Jesus as Lord and Savior. Whenever the heart believes, the veil is removed. Sight is no longer distorted but discovered!

Many times in my life I was guilty of putting a veil over truth. When the Holy Spirit began to speak to me about a ministry, I put a veil over it because I could not conceive it. All I could conceive was that I was a house wife from Indiana. And these thoughts were carried out in my actions. I had low self-esteem, a failure mentality, and I spoke doubt and unbelief, all of which are a rejection of the truth.

For me, it began to be resolved when I saw Jesus larger and greater and I saw that in the Word of God! Words are powerful. The Word of God is powerful.

> *And do not be conformed to this world,*
> *but be transformed by the renewing of*
> *your mind, that you may prove what is*
> *that good and acceptable and perfect*
> *will of God.*
>
> (Romans 12:2)

Transformation takes place in the heart and mind only through the power of God's Word. It seems that the Word of God is our only hope of renewing our thoughts, perceptions, and identity.

The Power of Words

It was with words that God created the Universe. He said, "Let there be light." And there was light and it was good. We believed in our hearts and confessed [words] that Jesus was Lord and we were saved. Words written on paper bind us to contracts we call loans. When we sign on the bottom line, we are agreeing to the terms of the contract. We are agreeing to repay the loan. At a wedding ceremony, words are spoken declaring the couple's intentions of a life long commitment.

My sister owns a wireless cellular phone company. When a person comes in to buy a cell phone, that person signs a service agreement for a one or two year term. If the agreement is broken, they will be fined some hefty charges. These signed papers protect her from constant loss in her business. They also provide her a legal foot to stand on if necessary.

We speak words in prayer, words which James (5:16) says makes great power available. Fervent, heart-felt words of prayer when coming from a person at peace with God, brings answers. Words must precede the power.

The Power of Thoughts

Eventually thoughts become words. In the last chapter we saw how our thoughts will locate us. We want to renew our minds and our thoughts before they become actions.

> *For as he thinks in his heart, so is he.*
> (Proverbs 23:7)

In Matthew 12:33-37, Jesus speaks about how a tree is known by its fruit. Upon further investigation of these verses, we realize that Jesus is speaking about thoughts and words.

> *For out of the abundance of the heart*
> *the mouth speaks.*
> (Matthew 12:34)

Jesus is telling us that whatever we store in our thoughts will come out. If we store good thoughts, the overflow will be good words. If we store evil thoughts, the overflow will be evil words. Our thought life is where we meditate. Impulses, urges, and ideas come from meditation. We need to make sure that what we store is the Word of God.

Let the word of Christ dwell in you richly in all wisdom, teaching and admonishing one another in psalms and hymns and spiritual songs, singing with grace in your hearts to the Lord.
(Colossians 3:16)

From this verse, we once again see the idea of overflow. A small quantity of the Word will not do. It must dwell in us in abundance. From the abundance, words of teaching, singing and admonition spill over.

There is a huge lake in my home town. When it rains for long periods of time, the lake fills beyond its capacity. The extra water overflows the concrete dam, and it runs down the spill-way like a mighty river. Like this lake, when we are full of the Word, we will pour out over others bringing refreshing and life.

Words Build Images

Words and thoughts carry a creative force. They enable us to see what may not be visible. For example, when I say the word "Empire State Building," you may have not ever visited there, but you *see* a large building. The building itself is not before you, but yet when I say its name, you can see its image in your mind.

I could also say, "My back hurts." When I do, it builds an image of pain. Or someone might say, "I am broke." Without realizing it, an image of lack and limitation begins to be built on the inside of that person.

Everyday our lives are surrounded by words spoken or thought. Have you ever said to someone, "I am so stupid, I would forget my head if it were not attached?" These words build an image of a person without any confidence. This image is impressed not only on the speaker's mind, but also the listener's mind. Remember how you see yourself is also how others will see you.

Have you ever spoken with someone on the phone and while hearing their voice, build an image of what they look like in your mind? Several years ago I had a bi-weekly radio broadcast. People would recognize my voice and usually ask me from where they knew me. When discovered it was from the radio, they would say, "Your voice doesn't match your face." What they were saying is, "You don't fit the image I built in my mind." If we can build images about people with our conversations, we can certainly do it with God and His Word. We have to change or rebuild the wrong images in our minds.

After seeing me in person, those people who had a wrong image of me were able to replace the wrong image with the true one. We have to do the same with God's Word for our spiritual lives. His Word does not change, our wrong perception has to.

Tearing Down the Wrong Image

If I were to ask you, "What does God look like?" How would you answer? If I were to poll 100 people, I would probably get 100 different answers. This is a very important question because if I am made in the image and likeness of God, then what am I supposed to look like?

As a young child, my image of God was one of a mean man holding a stick waiting for me to mess up so He could beat me. When I found that God was not like that, I would take the stick from His hand and beat myself. You may think that is a strange concept, but I figured that was what I deserved. I had a wrong image of God.

Through the Scriptures, I found out that God loved me. I found out He wasn't against me at all, He was actually for me. I began to see that God was not holding sin against me. When God the Father looked at me, He saw the blood. Revelation began to tear down the wrong image of God and rebuild the right one, a healthy one. The right image caused me to want to respond to Him, not run from Him.

In the same way, we have to renew our minds with the Word concerning ourselves. We have been taught not to think too highly of ourselves and this is Biblical, but it is just as detrimental to think of ourselves as worms. Because of Jesus, we are heirs of God, not worms.

If the wrong image can ever be torn down, and the right one built, people would press into their destinies and fulfill them.

> *For I know the thoughts and plans that*
> *I have for you, says the Lord, thoughts*
> *and plans for welfare and peace and*

> *not for evil, to give you hope in your*
> *final outcome.*
>   (Jeremiah 29:11, Amplified)

The enemy attacks the mind with thoughts and suggestions that constantly set us up for failure. As we have already seen, he uses the appetites of our flesh, to thwart the plans of God in our lives. One of his most successful ways is to build the wrong images on the inside of us. He accomplishes this by getting us to believe a lie.

Victory over a Wrong Image

Several years ago while I was visiting a woman minister in Missouri, something very powerful happened. A group of women and I, gathered together to seek the Lord. One particular morning this woman minister had a vision of me in a cage. It was not a big cage, but each bar of the cage represented words, staunch words spoken against me.

Inside the cage was a white dove between me and the door. Its wings were fluttering as if trying to get out. She then saw a hand coming with a key to unlock the door. After she shared this vision, I found myself lying on the floor under the power of the Holy Spirit.

I began remembering the staunch words spoken against me in the past. The words were flooding my mind: "You are an outspoken woman and you need to go home and find your place." Lying there, I vividly recalled the time a man once told me that God could not use me because I was too attractive.

Others told me God couldn't use me because I was female. Thoughts of being a high school drop out, a teen-age pregnant statistic, a house wife, mother, and an uneducated woman, made up the bars of this cage. This was my image. This was my identity.

While on the floor, the Holy Spirit began to speak to me about how the enemy was using a *type* of my anointing against me. Because I deeply desired to be used of the Lord and to speak words inspired by the Holy Ghost, the enemy was using words against me. I knew God had called me to be a prophetic voice with a passion to make Jesus real! I wanted my words to impart grace and life to those who heard. This was very important to me. The Holy Spirit spoke this scripture to me.

> *For the weapons of our warfare are not physical [weapons of flesh and blood], but they are mighty before God for the overthrow and destruction of strongholds, [Inasmuch as we] refute arguments and theories and reasonings and every proud and lofty thing that sets itself up against the [true] knowledge of God; and we lead every thought and purpose away captive into the obedience of Christ (the Messiah, the Anointed One).*
>
> (2 Corinthians 10:4-5, Amplified)

Instead, I was allowing the enemy to take me captive. The Lord gave me revelation that it was my duty and responsibility to take every thought, word, suggestion or imagination captive. He wanted me to cage the assaults of the enemy and throw away the key.

The vision accurately described how I saw myself. This was the image I had of myself: Bound and unable to be free. I realized my enemy was not the people who spoke these words; the enemy was my wrong perception of who I was. Again, I was allowing the opinions of people to define my identity.

The victory of this revelation has benefited me time and time again. The packaging the attacks come wrapped in differ and the attacks still come by words, but the purpose: To bind and weaken is the same. I have discovered it is not the messenger who is powerful, but the message the messenger carries. The gospel message has the power to bring deliverance and rescue! The power is in the Word.

True Biblical Confession

For many of us, due to our childhood and adult environment, the wrong image was built on the inside of us. As children, some heard how they were unwanted, just a mistake. For others the damaging words came from spouses, employers, grandparents, a teacher, or a coach. Even as Christians, we have heard hurtful words from others that have carried great influence. God wants these altars of idolatry torn down. We must begin to rebuild the right image of ourselves according to God and His Word.

True Biblical confession or agreement with the Word of God builds a right image inside us. It isn't mimicking words, it is *agreement* with truth. It's not just an imagined agreement, or hope, but agreement in faith. Faith comes when we can see God's will. His Word is His will.

The way the Lord showed it to me was like this. I can say, "I'm a truck. I'm a truck. I'm a truck, truck, truck," but that doesn't make me a truck. I can't *see* myself as a truck. I cannot see what I am confessing, so I cannot agree with it. On the other hand, confession or agreement with the Word of truth has the ability to paint a picture I can see. When I can see it, I can agree with it. Let us look at the difference. "I see a truck. I see a black Dodge Ram truck. I see a black Dodge Ram truck accented with silver chrome. I see a black Dodge Ram truck accented with silver chrome and a thousand dollar sound system that will give you a second heart beat." What just happened? You begin to see that truck in your mind, don't you?

> *"If you abide in My Word, you are My disciples indeed. And you shall know the truth, and the truth shall make you free."*
>
> (John 8:31-32)

The truth of God's Word liberates the mind from wrong thinking. It pulls down the old, dead images, and builds new, living ones. The Word allows us to not only have knowledge of the truth, but the person of Truth, Jesus Christ (John 14:6).

The ten spies who went into Canaan saw strong giants and large fortified cities and gave this bad report: "*And we were like grasshoppers in our own sight, and so we were in their sight*" (Numbers 13:33). This report was not untrue, it was misplaced. This image went against the Word of the Lord. Their instruction was to go in and possess the land because God had already given it to them. They were supposed to come in agreement with the Word of the Lord, the truth, not the facts that surrounded them.

> *And they spoke to all the congregation of the children of Israel, saying: "The land we passed through to spy out is an exceedingly good land. If the Lord delights in us, then He will bring us into this land and give it to us, a land which flows with milk and honey. Only do not rebel against the Lord, nor fear the people of the land, for they are our bread; their protection has departed from them, and the Lord is with us. Do not fear them."*
>
> (Numbers 14:7-9)

Joshua and Caleb were able to agree with the Word of the Lord. By placing their trust in the Lord, they could picture victory over the giants for the Lord was with them! Because they were able to see the victory, they were able to believe it. Their ability to believe was reflected in their confession: "*Let us go up at once and take possession, for we are well able to overcome it*" (Numbers 13:30).

> *But my servant Caleb, because he has a different spirit in him and has followed Me fully, I will bring him into the land where he went, and his descendants shall inherit it.*
>
> (Numbers 14:24)

This supernatural ability brought them the reward of fulfillment. They saw it by faith, believed God that they could possess it, and realized the promise.

> *But we all, with unveiled face, beholding as in a mirror the*
> *glory of the Lord, are being transformed into the same image*
> *from glory to glory, just as by the Spirit of the Lord.*
> 2 Corinthians 3:18

Chapter 6

Born-Again To Reflect

If we are going to clearly reflect our born-again identity, we are going to have to look at the right thing. We read in Genesis 1:26 where God said, "*Let Us make man in Our image, according to Our likeness.*" *In* could also be translated *as* (The Nelson Study Bible, p. 5). So it could be read, "Let Us make man *as* Our image."

It was said in ancient times that an emperor might have his statue put up in remote parts of his kingdom. These symbols would declare these areas were under his power and reign (The Nelson Study Bible, p. 5). In the same way, God intended man to be His living representatives who declare His reign. Therefore He said, "*Let them have dominion over all the earth.*"

Then God said, "*Let Us make man according to Our likeness.*" We are His images. We are to resemble the Lord. This places incredible value on people. We have been made to reflect His glory on the earth. Both male and female were created to reflect the image of God.

> *So God created man in His own image;*
> *in the image of God He created him;*
> *male and female He created them.*
>
> (Genesis 1:27)

To further explain this word *likeness*, let us look at Genesis 5:3. We find the same Hebrew use of the word. "*And Adam lived one hundred and thirty years, and begot a son in his own likeness, after his image, and named him Seth.*"

When a baby is born, how many times do we compare him to his parents? You will hear people say, "He has his mother's eyes." Or, "He is a spitting image of his father." This is what God created us to be, spitting images of our Father. I am amazed that God would choose mankind to be His representatives. How awesome! I feel a prayer wheel turning.

> *Dear Heavenly Father, we appreciate*
> *You. It is so wonderful to be made in*
> *Your image and likeness. Please help*
> *us to be holy representatives who*
> *accurately reflect the Biblical image*
> *of our Lord and Savior Jesus Christ.*
> *Remind us daily of this tremendous*
> *privilege. Empower us with Your*
> *Spirit of love and grace so that we*
> *may with anointing and power touch*

the human race, in the name of Jesus.
Amen.

Stolen Identity

Identity theft is a social concern of our day. Unfortunately it is not anything new. The devil initiated it thousands of years ago in the garden. Man, not angels (Satan is a fallen angel), was created to reflect the image and likeness of God. God formed Adam from the dust of the earth and then breathed into his nostrils the breath of God, and he became a living being or soul (Genesis 2:7). This personal touch and care distinguished him from all other living things. God personally got involved.

The word *formed* has the idea of a potter molding or shaping pots. Everything that God created, He created with a simple command. Man though was formed from dust. God then transformed the clay form into something *new*, by breathing His life into it. It, the clay form, was changed from one thing to another living thing, a man (The Nelson Study Bible, p. 7). I see this as a picture of the new birth.

When the serpent deceived Adam and Eve, He stole their identity. They had once enjoyed innocent fellowship with the Lord. Their thoughts and intentions were holy and pure. They were focused upon the Lord. They knew peace and walked blameless before their Creator. Now things were different. They were changed. They were not reflecting the glory the Lord intended for the two of them. They were running. They were hiding. Sin had entered the picture.

What does sin look like? Can we see it coming? In Genesis 3:6, the Bible says (after Eve's conversation with the serpent), she saw the tree "*was pleasant to the eyes, a tree desirable to make one wise.*" As previously mentioned, it does not appear that Eve had noticed the tree before this. Or at least, she was not tempted by it. This conversation contained a lie. Deception is a key the enemy uses to steal our identity. Lies move us from the truth, and deception builds the devils image rather than Gods.

It seems then, that sin is an invisible force affecting our, thoughts, imaginations, and even urges. Eve saw! Eve ate! Sin itself was invisible, but once it was acted upon, the results became visible. "*For the wages of sin is death. . .*" (Romans 6:23). Their eyes were opened and they knew they were naked (Genesis 2:7). They wanted and needed to be covered.

As earlier commented in chapter three, their minds were perhaps flooded with thoughts, accusations, and evil suggestions. The purpose was to move them from God-consciousness to self-consciousness. This brought distraction and destruction to their divine potential.

Dear readers, this is the grave danger of sin! When we sin, darkness is allowed into our lives. Adam and Eve's ability to reflect the Lord's glory was stolen. Remember the words of 2 Corinthians 3:18, "*But we all, with unveiled face, beholding as in a mirror, the glory of the Lord. . .*" A mirror can only reflect our image with the help of light. Their ability to reflect the glory of the Lord was hindered by sin. Their ability to reflect was swept away by the darkness. Every day we are kept from reflecting the image of our Lord Jesus Christ is a loss. This is the sad tragedy of being lost; there is failure to reflect or express the image and likeness of God. A reflection or expression that only that person can give!

Eve yielded to this invisible force. When she did, she did so with her physical body. Thoughts, suggestions, and urges were then carried out with her body. With her body she served the enemy. Our bodies are to be used for the Lord (1 Corinthians 6:13).

> *I beseech you therefore, brethren, by the mercies of God, that you present your bodies a living sacrifice, holy, acceptable to God, which is your reasonable service.*
>
> (Romans 12:1)

> *Or do you not know that your body is the temple of the Holy Spirit who is in you, whom you have from God, and you are not your own? For you were bought at a price; therefore glorify God in your body and in your spirit, which are God's.*
>
> (1 Corinthians 6:19-20)

We are a spirit. We have a soul; the seat of our emotions, our will, and our intellect. And we live in a body. It is God's desire that we fellowship with Him free from sin and distraction. The serpent appealed to Eve's soulish appetites and she gave in to them. The way to overcome the sinful desires of our carnal appetites is to consistently walk each and every step controlled by the Holy Spirit.

> *I say then: Walk in the Spirit, and you shall not fulfill the lust of the flesh. For the flesh lusts against the Spirit, and the Spirit against the flesh; and these are contrary to one another, so that you do not do the things that you wish. But if you are led by the Spirit, you are not under the law.*
>
> (Galatians 5:16-18)

Identity Restored

Jesus became God's answer for the problem. Just like the Lord made tunics of skin to cloth Adam and Eve, Jesus died to take away or abolish our sin. The old passes away and all things become new (2 Corinthians 5:17). Through His death, Jesus redeemed us and gave us a new identity. We are now heirs of God and joint-heirs with Jesus (Romans 8:17). He gave believers the right to become the children of God (John 1:12). It was pre-determined that believers would be conformed to the image of Jesus (Romans 8:29). There should be a change in our lives because we are being transformed into the likeness of Jesus Christ by the Spirit of the Lord (2 Corinthians 3:18).

*And do not be conformed to this world,
but be transformed by the renewing of
your mind, that you may prove what is
that good and acceptable and perfect
will of God.*

(Romans 12:2)

This word *transformed,* in both Romans 12:2 and 2 Corinthians 3:18, is the same Greek word. It is our English word metamorphosis meaning to change into another form. It signifies a complete change that will find expression in our character and conduct. It indicates a process stressing an inward and outward change (The New Strong's Expanded Exhaustive Concordance, p. 162). It will be accomplished by the Holy Spirit. His goal is that we be changed into the same image of Christ and live in moral excellence.

Through Jesus' victory on the cross and the power of the Holy Spirit, we can transform from a caterpillar to a butterfly.

The Holy Spirit quickens life in us and becomes a continual source of life. In the same way He breathed the breath of God into Adam, He quickened new life in us. *"It is the Spirit who gives life. . ."* (John 6:63). *". . . But the gift of God is eternal life in Christ Jesus our Lord"* (Romans 6:23).

Beholding the Lord's Glory

*But we all, with unveiled face,
beholding as in a mirror the glory of
the Lord, are being transformed into*

> *the same image from glory to glory,*
> *just as by the Spirit of the Lord.*
> (2 Corinthians 3:18)

Verse sixteen tells us that when we turn to the Lord, the veil is taken away. What was once hidden or covered is now revealed. It is now able to be seen. Verse seventeen says, *"Now the Lord is the Spirit; and where the Spirit of the Lord is, there is liberty."* Jesus' identity is reveled. Where the Spirit of the Lord is regenerating the heart, there is liberty. Jesus is no longer veiled or hidden. We are no longer blind and unable to see.

I heard the Lord say, "Where the Spirit of the Lord is, there is liberty; but where the Spirit of the Lord is not, there is no liberty, or freedom." Instead there is darkness and a veil. I often tell people, "Let the Lord deal with you." He will always bring freedom.

If the Spirit of the Lord is not at work regenerating your heart, won't you ask Him right now to come in? Just pray this prayer to God and mean it sincerely in your heart.

> *Dear God, I come to you a sinner. I*
> *need You to help me. I have made a*
> *mess of things trying to do it by myself.*
> *I believe in my heart that Jesus died*
> *on the cross for me. Wash me in Your*
> *precious blood. Come into my life*
> *and be my Lord and Savior. By faith, I*
> *believe I am forgiven, I am saved, and*
> *I confess Jesus is my Lord.*

Perhaps you once asked Jesus to come into your heart, but sin has separated you, and now the Holy Spirit is dealing with you. Won't you invite Him back into your heart today? Now is the accepted time, today is the day of salvation.

> *Today, if you will hear His voice, do not harden your hearts.*
> (Hebrews 3:7-8)

> *Dear God, I have allowed other things to come before You. I have let the things I have heard and learned slip away. Please forgive me. Cleanse me with the precious blood of your Son. I purpose to make a fresh dedication of my life to You. Come into my heart and be my Lord and Savior. I receive Your forgiveness and Your mercy. I confess that Jesus is my Lord.*

The word *beholding* means to mirror one-self, i.e. to see reflected (The New Strong's Expanded Exhausted Concordance, p. 34). What are you beholding? We are to behold the glory of the Lord according to 2 Corinthians 3:18. This word *glory* indicates an ever-growing opinion and the honor that results from that good opinion (The New Strong's Expanded Exhaustive Concordance, p. 70).

God's glory is manifested in His nature and His acts. His character and His ways were exhibited through Jesus. As we see them reflected, we not only obtain a visible picture of the Lord, but also awe, honor and respect. This describes intimacy.

Through this on-going intimacy, we are being transformed or changed into the same image we are beholding. We are becoming different. We are being developed to resemble the Lord. We become His representatives to the world and we declare His Lordship. As we reflect Him, His glory is manifested.

From Glory To Glory

If God's glory is the manifestation of His character, nature, and ways, then how does it come? It comes through revelation; the Spirit's ability to make Jesus known.

As the Spirit reveals Jesus to us, especially through the Word, our opinion and knowledge of Him grows. As our knowledge of Him grows, so does our reverence. Reverence brings honor and worship, proper responses to all that He has done and given us.

> *For in Him dwells all the fullness of the God-head bodily; and you are complete in Him, who is the head of all principality and power.*
> (Colossians 2:9-10)

All the fullness of God resides in Jesus! Nothing needs to be added to what we have already received in Jesus. It just needs to be uncovered.

Upon further study of these verses, I discovered a tremendous revelation. The phrase *"fullness of the God-head"* means "totality" (The Nelson Study Bible, p. 2016). Jesus, then, is the sum total of the divine nature of God! Math being my favorite subject, the word "sum" stuck out to me. Sum is the answer to an addition problem. Since numbers are infinite, meaning we can always add one more, I began to understand a depth of Jesus never before realized. Many statements in the Bible seem to express a depth in the Lord not yet discovered. Statements are made about the "unsearchable riches" of Christ, the "hidden treasures" of wisdom and knowledge, and the need to "grow" in grace and knowledge.

Paul prayed prayers asking the Lord to reveal the depths of His love, His purpose, and His wisdom to the saints.

> *That the God of our Lord Jesus Christ, the Father of glory, may give to you the spirit of wisdom and revelation in the knowledge of Him, the eyes of your understanding being enlightened; that you may know what is the hope of His calling, what are the riches of the glory of His inheritance in the saints, and what is the exceeding greatness of His power toward us who believe, according to the working of His mighty power.*
>
> (Ephesians 1:17-19)

> *That He would grant you, according to the riches of His glory, to be strength-*

> *ened with might through His Spirit in*
> *the inner man, that Christ may dwell*
> *in your hearts through faith; that you,*
> *being rooted and grounded in love,*
> *may be able to comprehend with all*
> *the saints what is the width and length*
> *and depth and height, to know the*
> *love of Christ which passes knowl-*
> *edge; that you may be filled with all*
> *the fullness of God.*
>
> (Ephesians 3:16-19)

My pastor used to always say, "You have as much of Jesus as you want." Most of us don't like that statement because the responsibility comes back to us. There is so much more! Do you want to know how I know? The Bible tells me that the ones who hunger and thirst for righteousness shall be filled! (Matthew 5:6). I know there is more because I am not satisfied yet. In Jesus, there is plenty! The number 253,007, can be added to; 253,008, 253,009, 253,010. . .it just keeps going.

Jesus is the same way; He continues to reveal one facet after another about Himself! He just keeps getting larger and larger. It has been said of the four living creatures, full of eyes in front and in back who are all around the throne of God, that they do not rest. This is due to the holiness of God they continually behold (Revelation 4:6-8). Every time they look at Jesus, they see something they never saw before. I am not sure if this is true, but the principle of plenitude is definitely found in the Scriptures.

There have been many times in my life when I have cried out to the Lord, "I need you to turn for me Jesus! I need to see You in a way I have not seen before. I need to realize a dimension of You that will strengthen and encourage my heart." He has never failed me. He continually takes me from one view of glory to another.

> *To the intent that now the manifold wisdom of God might be made known by the church to the principalities and powers in the heavenly places.*
> (Ephesians 3:10)

> *O Lord, how manifold are Your works! In wisdom You have made them all.*
> (Psalm 104:24)

The word manifold in Ephesians indicates variety, diversity or variegated (The New Strong's Expanded Exhaustive Concordance, p. 206). We see this principle in creation. No two people look exactly the same. Everyone has a different finger print. Since God made mankind as His image this reveals His variety and diverseness. No two snowflakes look the same. There are no two animals that look alike. Every tree is different and distinct. The birds of the air are uniquely different as well as the fish of the sea.

The word *manifold* in the Old Testament means "to cast together, i.e. increase, especially in number" (The New Strong's Expanded Exhaustive Concordance, p. 256). This signifies abundance, many, or large. It means plural in number or amount. The Psalmist spoke of God's abundant and tender mercies (Psalm 106:45; Psalm 69:16). Nehemiah spoke of His many mercies to the Israelites in the wilderness; the cloud by day and the pillar of fire by night to show them the way to go (9:19).

Wow! What a mighty, awesome God we serve! He just keeps revealing Himself to us, and we just keep growing and growing. We go from glory to glory, or from one good opinion to another good opinion allowing us to consistently reflect His like- ness to the world.

But as it is written:
"Eye has not seen, nor ear heard, nor have
entered into the heart of man the things
which God has prepared for those who love
Him." But God has revealed them to us
through His Spirit. For the Spirit searches
all things, yes, the deep things of God.
1 Corinthians 2:9-10

Chapter 7

Transformation
by the Spirit

Beholding the glory of the Lord has to do with our intimacy with Him. Through intimacy the Holy Spirit changes us into the image of Christ. The Bible tells us the Holy Spirit was sent to be our Helper (John 14:26). He was given to lead us and guide us into truth (John 16:13). His job is to make Jesus known (John 16:14).

It seems then, that revelation precedes transformation. Paul thought he was doing the right thing by persecuting Christians (Acts 9:1-2). But he was knocked from his perch of ignorant unbelief and then began a new life of transformation (Acts 9:4). His own testimony was that he was the chief of sinners (1 Timothy 1:15). Afterward, he was baptized in the Holy Spirit (Acts 9:27). We know this included speaking in tongues, for Paul said, *"I thank my God, I speak with tongues more than you all"* (1 Corinthians 14:18).

Many people fight the baptism in the Holy Spirit. They argue it is not for us today. Others determine it is only for the elite. First of all, I would like to remind us that the baptism in the Holy Spirit is not *just* tongues; it is an experience with the Holy Spirit! It is an endowment of power for the purpose of witnessing (Acts 1:8). It is being immersed in life and power. It is an impartation of life (John 6:63). It is a love encounter with the person of the Holy Spirit. Tongues, then, is the initial evidence of that life (Acts 2:4).

People often ask me why I believe in the Holy Spirit so much. My answer is because Jesus wants me to have it. In Luke 24:49, Jesus said, *"Behold, I send the Promise of My Father upon you; but tarry in the city of Jerusalem until you are endued with power from on high."* The baptism in the Holy Spirit was Jesus' intention for all who would believe upon His name. It was necessary to receive this Promise before going into the whole world to fulfill the Great Commission. It was Jesus' command not to go until power had been received from above! Some argue it was only for the Apostles, but there were a hundred and twenty in the Upper Room that day (Acts 1:15) and *all* of them were filled!

Transformation Starts with Power

In Acts 1:8, Jesus told the disciples that they would receive power after the Holy Spirit came upon them.

The Holy Spirit brings power or ability into our lives. This miraculous force is at work in us. His ability residing on the inside of us brings transformation.

Paul is a wonderful example of this. He was dragging people off to prison who were of the Way. He consented to Stephen's death (Acts 8:1). Verse three says, "*He made havoc of the church.*" This phrase is likened to the description of a wild bore stampeding with the intent to destroy whatever is in its path (The Nelson Study Bible, p. 1832).

Revelation preceded Paul's transformation. Ananias was sent to tell Paul the things that would happen to him (Acts 9:15-16). His call was explained to him. Prayer was offered not only for him to receive his sight but to be filled with the Holy Spirit. Acts 9:18 says, "*Immediately there fell from his eyes something like scales, and he received his sight at once; and he arose and was baptized. Immediately he preached the Christ in the synagogues, that He is the Son of God*" (Acts 9:20). Paul as well as the disciples needed the baptism in the Holy Spirit before beginning their ministries.

The word "endued" in Luke 24:49 has the idea of slipping into a new set of clothes (The New Strong's Expanded Exhaustive Concordance, p. 88). So when Jesus said, "*be endued with power,*" He was saying, "sink into a new garment and you will be clothed with power." Just as Adam and Eve needed to be clothed, we need to be clothed.

We see the same idea in Ephesians 6:11 where Paul told believers to "put on" the whole armor of God; it was the only way to be protected from the strategies of the devil. Slipping into a new set of clothes is necessary in order to withstand in the evil day. When Jesus said to the disciples in Acts 1:8, *"But you will receive power when the Holy Spirit has come upon you,"* He was telling them the new garment was the Holy Spirit.

The Armor of God

I have always thought of the knight's armor when reading these verses in Ephesians chapter six. When we step into the garment of the Spirit's power, we are protected and able. Again, Jesus said this was necessary before starting any ministry.

> *In conclusion, be strong in the Lord [be empowered through your union with Him]; draw your strength from Him [that strength which His boundless might provides].*
> (Ephesians 6:10, Amplified)

Our strength comes from the Lord. We are made strong through our union with Him. This union is the intimacy we have with Him. Earlier we shared from John 15:5 where Jesus said, *"I am the vine, you are the branches. He who abides* (disappears by sinking into) *Me, and I in him, bears much fruit; for without Me you can do nothing."* As long as we are connected to the Lord, we are able to draw life and strength from Him. Apart from Him however, we are not able to do anything.

Through the intimacy of the Holy Spirit (speaking in tongues and worship), great revelation comes. The Holy Spirit is the one who enables! This is why Jesus thought it was necessary for us to receive Him.

Several years ago, I was challenged by my minister friend from Oklahoma to spend one year in special prayer. Several ladies and I met every Thursday for two hours and just spent time praying in the Spirit. Some weeks you could hear cries and sobs, and other weeks there was great rejoicing in worship, but each and every week there was intimacy with the Holy Ghost. I would walk the floors of my house saying, "Lord, You open doors no man can shut. You shut doors no man can open. I thank you that doors are opening to me in the North, the South, the East and the West." I wanted so desperately to get out there and get with it, but the truth was I needed to be endued with power from on high. This time of intimacy with the Holy Spirit brought confidence, courage, and ability, and doors opened too.

One opened in Evansville, IN. I will never forget it. I was preaching in a small church and by the Spirit I said one night, "I believe I will go to nations." What? Who said that? I was terrified. As the words came out of my mouth, fear gripped my heart. I realized that I did not say it, the Holy Ghost did! And guess what? He brought it to pass.

Being born into this world allows us to touch the natural realm, and being born again and filled with the Holy Spirit allows us to touch the supernatural. The supernatural is God's power and ability. From this ability, life flows. The Holy Spirit is the bridge to intimacy with the Lord.

The Lord spoke to me and said, "It is imperative that you fellowship with the Holy Spirit." He is your Helper, Comforter, Counselor, Intercessor, Strengthener, Standby, and Advocate (John 14:26, Amplified). As the Lord gave Eve to Adam, He gave the Holy Spirit to us. It was not good that we be alone (John 14:18).

Transformation Follows Revelation

Through our intimacy with the Holy Spirit comes glorious revelation.

> *But as it is written: "Eye has not seen, nor has ear heard, nor have entered into the heart of man the things which God has prepared for those who love Him." But God has revealed them to us through His Spirit. For the Spirit searches all things, yes, the deep things of God. For what man knows the things of a man except the spirit of the man which is in him? Even so no one knows the things of God except the Spirit of God. Now we have received, not the spirit of the world, but the Spirit who is from God, that we might know the things that have been freely given to us by God.*
>
> (1 Corinthians 2:9-12)

When the Holy Spirit spoke to me that I would go to nations, I could not understand how, when, or why. After all, I was just a housewife from Indiana. The Holy Spirit *knew* the mind of God. Through intimacy, I knew His will too. Since I was a little girl, I had a burning desire to travel, and I didn't know where it came from. I wanted to be an airline stewardess, a truck driver (believe me, it is a long story), and even a traveling business woman. And now, the Holy Spirit was revealing to me what God had planned for my life. God is faithful, and has allowed me the opportunity to travel to 13 countries. I am thankful and I give Him the glory! He wants to do great things, and He wants to do them through you. God is not hiding His will from you He is reserving it for you. God wants you to know the things He has prepared for you. They are hidden in the Spirit. When we fellowship with the Holy Spirit, He makes them known to us.

Paul received revelation by the Spirit. In Ephesians 3:3, 5 he says, "*How that by revelation He made known to me the mystery, which in other ages was not made known to the sons of men, as it has now been revealed by the Spirit to His holy apostles and prophets.*" We know that Paul was in fellowship with the Holy Spirit and that he prayed in the Spirit. I do not believe the church has yet tapped in to the power and purpose of praying in other tongues. Revelation knowledge of the church transformed Paul's entire life. Further revelation enabled him to write two-thirds of the New Testament.

In Romans 8:26-27, Paul states that the Holy Spirit helps us in our weaknesses. We do not know what to pray for but the Holy Spirit does and He makes intercession for us according to the will of God for our lives.

Paul said in 1 Corinthians 14:2 that when we speak in tongues, we are praying to God; we are speaking mysteries. Verse 13 tells us that when we speak in tongues, we should pray that we may interpret. I believe this is what happened when I said by the Spirit I would go to nations. All those months of prayer brought revelation knowledge concerning my future.

Jude 19 reveals to us that sense ruled people are those without the Spirit. But verses 20-21 declare, *"But you, beloved, building yourselves up on your most holy faith, praying in the Holy Spirit, keep yourselves in the love of God, looking for the mercy of the Lord Jesus Christ unto eternal life."*

Revelation comes by the Holy Spirit to our spirit. It doesn't make sense to the mind. As a matter of fact, we can talk ourselves out of a lot of things God has for us because we simply can't figure out the details with our mind. Praying in the Spirit has a way of shutting down our minds. Paul stated that when we pray in a tongue, our spirit prays but our mind or understanding is unfruitful (1 Corinthians 14:14). Praying in the Spirit keeps us in faith which is a requirement to pleasing God (Hebrews 11:6) and keeps cultivating a love for God. It lifts us up from a natural perspective to a supernatural perspective. We are edified or built up like a high rise building climbing higher and higher.

Thank God, He didn't leave us alone! He gave us help and ability to do all He created us to do.

Transformation Is Growth

Transformation comes through growing pains. Growth is the result of revelation. Growth is obedience to God's ways and His will that have been revealed by His Spirit. It is personal, practical, and a process. Sometimes it is a painful process but it produces the peaceable fruit of righteousness. Each stage of growth brings us closer to the image of Christ. God's plan for our lives is that we grow in grace from one level of glory to another.

Peter serves as a good example. His name, Simon, meant wishy-washy; but Jesus gave him a new name, Peter which meant rock. He would be a foundation stone used in building the church, although he denied Jesus and cowered in the background refusing to be identified with the Lord. When the rooster crowed, revelation pierced his heart. He repented and from that experience he grew. A few days later he was empowered by the Holy Spirit, preached to a crowd of people, and three thousand were saved. He was once a coward, but now he was a bold minister for Jesus. He was transformed by the Holy Spirit.

And Peter remembered the word of Jesus who said to him, "Before the rooster crows, you will deny me three times." So he went out and wept bitterly.
(Matthew 26:75)

We have a tendency to want transformation without growth. Growing in Christ is hard because it requires change. We are forced to look at our lives with complete honesty. Growth demands progress and transformation comes when we walk through the hard things.

This painful experience had to be faced in Peter's life. Peter genuinely repented, and in John 21, we read that Jesus restored him. Every time Jesus asked Peter, "Do you love Me?" I believe he grew. Jesus would not allow him to run from his past. As he faced it, Jesus healed him. Peter then writes about the revelations learned through grievous trials in the two books that bear his name. He testifies to the fact that we are kept by the power of God. In this wonderful gift of salvation we rejoice, but due to the hardships of life, we experience grief (1 Peter 1:5-6).

James tells us to count it all joy when you go through hard things. It develops a staying power in our life. It builds endurance that enables us to stand up under the pressure of the trial. It builds spiritual muscles if you will.

Some of the things I have already shared with you made me want to bow under the pressure and difficulty. It was the Spirit's ability that kicked in and kept me from quitting. God has given us everything we need to win. Every hardship I have gone through was extremely painful to me, but looking back, I would not trade any one of the experiences for an easy way out. They have made me who I am today. We must remember that He is the potter, we are just the clay. He is molding us into His image.

The writer of Hebrews gives us this encouragement, *"Let us run with endurance the race that is set before us, looking unto Jesus, the author and finisher of our faith"* (Hebrews 12:1-2). He goes on to say that when we become weary we are to think about all that Jesus endured. We are reminded that Jesus will chasten the ones He loves. It isn't pleasant. As a matter of fact, it is painful. It is intended to train us in righteousness.

If you abide in My Word, you are My disciples indeed.
And you shall know the truth, and the truth shall make you free.
John 8:31-32

Chapter 8

Transformation through the Word

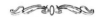

In John 8:31-32, Jesus is saying to believers, "If you hold fast to My Word (My teachings and obey them), you are true disciples." The one who abides, remains, and continues in the Word of God knows the truth. The truth will deliver you from the bondage of sin.

Up to this point, I was still in training. Although I was doing some teaching and preaching, I wanted to flow in a greater anointing. I knew the anointing destroyed the yokes of bondage, but the question remained, how do I get there? I was also learning that everything was in the Lord's timing. I would cry out, "When God, when? How long Lord, how long?" The same answer would always come, "Until." I began to wonder if there was something I needed to be doing while I was waiting for the fulfillment of the things

I believed for. Was there something that would help me to get from point A to point B?

The Lord was certainly developing my character. I was discovering that while I was learning to trust Him, He was watching to see if He could trust me.

In Hebrews five, the writer exhorts us to mature. He speaks about Jesus' spiritual development. He learned obedience through the things He suffered (5:8). His experience on the cross, when completed, qualified Him to be the Author of eternal life. He was equipped with authority to offer salvation to everyone who would hear and obey (v.9).

Verse eleven speaks about those, who, unlike Jesus, were not responding to the Word of God. They were not quick to accept it but were becoming lazy in achieving spiritual insight. It became hard to speak to them due to being sluggish (The Nelson Study Bible, p. 2084, 2085). Sometimes, we do not hear the voice of God because we have become "*dull of hearing.*" If it was happening to them, it can happen to us.

The problem was they were not progressing. They were remaining babies. I realized that in order for Jesus to trust me with the anointing, I was going to have to become skilled in the Word of righteousness. I needed to grow up and achieve some spiritual insight of my own.

> *For everyone who partakes* (continues to feed) *only of milk is unskilled in the Word of righteousness, for he is a babe. But solid food belongs to those who are full age, that is, those who by*

> *reason of use have their senses exer-*
> *cised to discern both good and evil.*
>   (Hebrews 5:13-14)

The Word Makes You Wise

I wanted to be "full age." I had an insatiable desire to be spiritually mature. According to the above verses, it was my choice. I could continue to drink milk (hear and not learn) or I could practice what the Word told me to do. Those who make it a habit to obey the truth will mature in their faith. Mature faith can distinguish between good and evil.

Paul warned Timothy that in the last days, men would resist the truth. The result; corrupt minds and disapproved faith (2 Timothy 3:8). Paul announces, *"but they will progress no further"* (v.9). Progress then is directly related to a proper response to the truth, the Word of God.

Paul further encouraged Timothy in 2 Timothy 3:14-15: *"But you must continue in the things which you have learned and been assured of, knowing from whom you have learned them, and that from childhood you have known the Holy Scriptures, which are able to make you wise for salvation through faith which is in Christ Jesus."*

These words of encouragement were written to Timothy after detailing the perilous times of the last days. Notice the type of people who made the list: the boastful, the proud, lovers of pleasure, the selfish, the greedy, those full of pride, the unthankful, those without love, those unwilling to forgive, and the headstrong. It seems then, that the Word is the antidote for the list in 2 Timothy 3:1-7. In verse six, Paul relayed that the deception of the last days would hit those loaded down with sins and those led away by all kinds of lusts. Why? Verse seven offers the answer, "*always learning and never able to come to the knowledge of the truth.*"

We have to have an ear to hear the truth of the Bible. We also must have a receptive heart to obey and practice the things we learn. Living in the truth of the Scriptures should be a daily habit that we develop.

New Direction

When we really hear, there will be a change in the way we think and live. There is understanding of what Jesus wants for our lives. As our minds are renewed, our lives take on a new direction. We soon realize our thoughts and perceptions do not agree with the Lord. Agreement with truth brings the blessings!

Do you remember when Joshua and Caleb agreed with the Lord? They agreed they were able to take the land in spite of the giants. The word given to them was God's will. Although it took years, it was proven to them and fulfilled.

Like the ten spies, most of us spent our past life looking at half truths and lies. The way we thought was how we lived and conducted ourselves. We were sinners and we thought sin was okay and even fun. Our actions proved our sinfulness. In the same way, when our mind is renewed, our actions prove we are in right standing with God.

When I would look at myself, I saw failure and insecurity. By looking into the Word I began to agree with the truth. I began to see I could be a new person. I began to see the person God wanted me to be.

James writes that we are to *receive* the Word of God into our lives. We are to be open and teachable. When we are teachable, the Word is sown into our hearts (James 1:21). As the psalmist said, *"Your Word I have hidden in my heart, that I might not sin against You"* (Psalm 119:11). The Word contains power to save our souls. The Word gives us life, purpose, and new direction! James gives further instruction. He tells us it is not enough to just hear the Word, we must apply it to our lives. We must obey it. The one who does not take action after hearing the Word is likened to a man looking into a mirror. After walking away, he forgets what he saw (James 1:22-24). In other words, nothing is reflected.

> *But he who looks into the perfect law of liberty and continues in it, and is not a forgetful hearer but a doer of the work, this one is blessed in what he does.*
>
> (James 1:25)

In this verse, James is telling us that when we receive the Word with a teachable spirit, it is very important that action immediately follow. For example, when I heard that the Word taught the principle of tithing, I immediately began to tithe. I received the Word and then responded. Tithing, then, became a part of my life. Because immediate action followed what I had heard, it was hard to forget what the Word said to do. The Word brought transformation to my finances.

Transformation comes to every area of our lives in the same way. When the Word of God speaks truth to us, we are required to act on that truth. As we do, it takes root in our life. It will bring forth change and life will come forth. There will be a new focus in an entirely different direction.

Transformed By Truth

When Jesus said, *"And you shall know the truth, and the truth shall make you free"* (John 8:32), He was saying truth is greater than facts. Truth was greater than the facts of Paul's life. Truth was greater than the facts of my life, and truth is greater than the facts of your life.

Paul *was* a blasphemer, an insolent man. He was full of self-righteous learning, but the truth was he was called by God to preach the gospel. He was chosen to display the grace of God. He was also told he would have to suffer. Paul agreed with this truth and spent the rest of his life walking in it. This was only the beginning; more truth was given in spite of the facts of his past. Hallelujah!

In my life, the facts were teen-age pregnant statistic and high school drop out. I was plagued by a failure mentality. God knew all of that when He called me. God knows where you have been, but He has something greater to say about it. Somewhere in our walk with God, we have to begin to renew our minds and agree with the truth. The truth is His Word, the Bible, and the things He speaks to your own spirit. We will not possess the promises of God until we learn how to agree with Him. Things do not just fall on us, they are given or offered to us, but we have to receive them.

When the Lord spoke to my heart to go to Bible College, no one knocked on my door saying, "Gloria Kramer, you are the next candidate to receive credentials from the Assemblies of God." No, I had to study, take tests, and pass the courses. It was available, but I had to do the work.

The Word of God is living and very powerful, but sitting on the shelf of your study, it is powerless. According to Ephesians 6:17, when we take the Word that is given to us in a time of need, it becomes like a sword. It is a powerful weapon. All the Israelites heard the gospel but all of them did not profit from it. They did not mix faith with what they heard (Hebrews 4:2). Hearing the Word and mixing faith with it is the key. If we are to receive or profit, we must agree or believe what the Lord is saying to us. The Israelites could not conceive what they had heard. Therefore, they would not agree with it. So, they died in that old dusty wilderness when it was God's will to bring them into the land He promised.

Romans 12:2 tells us that renewing our mind is essential. It proves or authenticates God's will for our lives. The Bible says in Philippians 4:19, "*And my God shall supply all your need according to His riches in glory by Christ Jesus.*" The facts of my life may say, "broke," "hopeless," and "helpless," nevertheless, it is God's will to meet my needs. As I have agreed with this promise, I have experienced the proof in my life!

Paul was going the wrong direction. The Most High had to turn him around. Most of us need Him to turn us around too. Paul had an encounter with Jesus on the road to Damascus where the Lord called him. He received His instructions from the Lord, and He validated him. After his conversion, he got away for a period of three years (Galatians 1:18). Personally, I think it was a time of fellowship and training. We know that Paul received great revelation from the Lord. The time spent with the Lord was necessary for him to receive revelation. Every minister I know had a time of preparation, a time of study; a unique period of time spent with the Lord. Paul had his, I had mine, and you will have yours.

Personal Transformation

The Lord was calling me to set aside time to study, but because I was married and had three children, I could not go away to Bible school. I enrolled in Berean College, a Bible correspondence school out of Springfield, Missouri. In two years, I completed sixteen Bible courses. He was calling me to a time of training in the school of the Holy Spirit. He was requiring me to grow up. He was directing me on how I would reach a new level in the ministry He had called me to. He was initiating spiritual achievement. He was demanding that I not become sluggish. I was being asked to progress.

Over the next two years, I studied eight to nine hours a day. I would put my children on the school bus and head upstairs to my comfortable plaid recliner, which became my friend. Even though I had text books, I would get off on my own studies. I would follow bunny trails so to speak. This proved to be a marvelous time of grace upon my life. It was a divinely appointed time. I am thankful for it. It was an appointment that needed to be kept. I was full of passion to learn from the Lord. I felt like Mary sitting each day at the feet of Jesus hearing His words! I literally had to be dragged away. My children would come home and be hungry. I struggled to move. They would come up and ask when I was going to fix dinner. I would say, "In a minute." My minute would turn into another hour. I found it so hard to stop. I know it was supernatural. I owe a great debt to my family for allowing me to have such an opportunity.

My heartbeat was to become "full age," skilled in the Word of righteousness, able to rightly divide the Word of truth. I was consumed with desire to be wise in my salvation experience.

> *Be diligent to present yourself approved to God, a worker who does not need to be ashamed, rightly dividing the Word of truth.*
>
> (2 Timothy 2:15)

Timothy was a young pastor, just starting in the ministry. Paul, under the inspiration of the Holy Spirit, thought it was necessary to strengthen this young minister and help him to understand the importance of study.

During this time of study, the Word was being sown in my life. Seeds were being sown that would bring a great harvest in the years to come. This time of study brought great transformation to my life. Understanding was coming. Revelation was transpiring. Confidence was arising. My crippled mentality was being transformed. Failure was fading away. Vision was penetrating the wall of past mistakes and wrong identity. It was a fruitful time in my life.

> *For the Word of God is living and powerful, and sharper than any two-edged sword, piercing even to the division of soul and spirit, and of joints and marrow, and is a discerner of the thoughts and intents of the heart.*
>
> (Hebrews 4:12)

An Approved Worker

When Paul told Timothy to be diligent to present himself "approved," he was implying what remains after testing, like metals that have been refined by fire (The Nelson Study Bible, p. 2058). What comes through testing is found approved.

Faith goes through tests. The Bible says in Romans 10:17, *"So then faith comes by hearing, and hearing by the Word of God.*" I can testify that faith continues to grow by studying the Word of God. After all of this study, I went through some tremendous tests.

I was teaching in my church, and other opportunities were opening for me to minister, but mostly as a teacher. The Lord had confirmed the call to preach. I had spent time in study, and now my first official invitation had come to preach in a small church in a nearby city.

I was so blessed by the way the invitation came, I did not see it as a test. My husband was the best man in his army buddy's wedding. We were at this church for that purpose. After the ceremony, we met the pastor. He asked my husband if he was a minister (that happened a lot), his reply was, "No, but my wife is." The pastor seemed a little surprised.

We talked a few minutes, and then he asked me if I would come the next night to preach. I was so excited! At last! He left me feeling confident as he responded to my question, "Are you sure?" His reply, "I would rather see a woman minister who is on fire preach the Word, than a man minister it in deadness."

The next morning while at church, I had my pastor pray for me. After getting my children some lunch, I shut myself in to pray and seek the Lord. I heard these words, "The devil means this for harm, but I mean it for good." Wait a minute! What is that supposed to mean? "Lord, You can't say that to me without an explanation," I whined, but no explanation came. For three hours that afternoon, I prayed in the Holy Ghost. I was a little apprehensive about going, but I had made a commitment.

When I arrived, the army buddy's wife met me at the door. She told me that the pastor wanted to see me in his office. I was really nervous now. He asked me to sit down so I did. He tells me he was having second thoughts and that he might have made a mistake in inviting me. I was crushed. I sat there for a few seconds (it felt like minutes), and then these words came from me, "You are the pastor of this church and I will submit myself to your authority, but I have come here tonight with a word from the Lord." I don't know who was more shocked – me or him. He hesitated for a little while, and then he responded, "Sister, please take your liberty." What? How am I supposed to do that? The whole situation was pounding my mind with so many thoughts. All my insecurities were resurrecting.

Thank God for the hour worship service! I was able to mentally work through all the "stuff" that had just happened. I quoted myself every scripture I could think of. Then it came time to take the pulpit. As soon as the pastor introduced me, he made his way to the back of the church and stood with his back against the wall. He also raised one foot and placed it against the wall. I was so intimidated. He would not even sit down, but I kept my heart right before the Lord. I do not know if it was wisdom, but I started the sermon by saying there are people who don't think a woman ought to stand here. I went on to clarify my position was in Christ, and that He had given me a message to speak that night.

After preaching the service, the Lord worked with me manifesting the gifts of the Spirit. Something new happened. Something had changed. The gift of the word of knowledge was flowing with such grace and ease. It was as if I were watching myself on video. It seemed surreal, but it was great!

A New Beginning

I had been praying for it. I had desired the anointing for as long as I could remember. I was *really* walking in the anointing. It was like nothing I had experienced at this level. It felt so good! Finally!

There were several things that really struck me that night. A woman came for prayer that I had never met before. As I laid my hands on her, these words came out of my mouth, "You're a teacher, aren't you?" She nodded and then the tears began to flow. She would tell me later that she had been in to talk with her pastor about teaching in the church but she was not received. It was as if the Lord was lifting her up, and confirming her. Then there was a man who came for prayer. Because I was so scared of doing something wrong, I kept my hands on his raised hands where everyone could see them. As I touched his hands, I prayed this prayer. "Lord, bless the work of this man's hands. Let all that he touches prosper." He came up to me after the service that night and handed me his business card. I could not believe my eyes when I saw that he was cabinet maker. Several other men came and asked *me* to pray for them. I was so humbled. Words can't describe all the emotions I felt that night.

The Lord had sent me to speak. The Word was preached, and signs and wonders followed (Mark 16:20). Truly the Lord did mean it for my good. He honored me that night, but more importantly, He honored His Word!

Faith and Patience

Waiting for something from the Lord can be excruciating! The Lord definitely does not seem to keep the same time we do. We grow impatient. Sometimes we grow weary. At times, we can even grow angry. I have found an answer.

> *That you do not become sluggish, but imitate those who through faith and patience inherit the promises.*
> (Hebrews 6:12)

Constancy is a key to not becoming sluggish or slothful. We learn from this verse, that believers were challenged to keep before them the example of those who had persevered. By doing so, promises would be fulfilled and enjoyed. Faith and patience need to be copied. Those who have already received fulfillment to their promises need to be imitated. Just as the writer of Hebrews communicated this truth to his audience, we should also hear and learn. It is so easy to lose our focus while we are waiting for the promises to be granted to us.

Trust is crucial. Trust in the faithfulness of God's Word brings transformation. It not only transforms us, but things around us. Hebrews chapter eleven gives testimony of many who placed their trust in the Lord. Each individual was transformed. Moses was one example. In verse 27, we are told he forsook Egypt. He found ability to endure by *seeing* the invisible God. His faith caused circumstances that surrounded him and his people to be transformed. They passed through the Red Sea on dry land, but when the Egyptians attempted to cross, they drowned.

Through faith and patience, Joshua and Caleb received their allotment of land (Joshua 14:6-15). In verse seven, Caleb reminisces about the promise given more than forty years earlier. He declared in verse eight, "*but I wholly followed the Lord my God.*"

Caleb continues to testify about God's faithfulness. He kept him alive forty-five years, as strong as the day he spied out the land of Canaan. Joshua then hands him the deed to his mountain. The Bible says it like this, "*Hebron therefore became the inheritance of Caleb the son of Jephunneh the Kenizzite to this day, because he wholly followed the Lord God of Israel*" (v.14). I would say forty-five years qualifies as patience. Caleb's faith was just as strong on the day he received his inheritance as it was the day it was promised. What faith! What patience!

Let me encourage you, God can not lie. He is faithful and true and what He has promised you, He will do. Stay focused. Remain strong. You will receive! Let the Word of God bring transformation to you and your life, especially during the waiting time.

Something that has helped me tremendously is to keep what I call a "word book." This book contains all the promises God has personally spoken to me. I regularly take it out and read it to bring to my remembrance the unfulfilled promises of God, especially when I have been waiting a long time. It reminds me that God is trustworthy as I acknowledge the promises already fulfilled. This generally adds new fervor to any impatience I might be experiencing.

> *God is not a man, that He should lie, nor a son of man, that he should repent. Has He said, and will He not do? Or has He spoken, and will He not make it good?*
>
> (Numbers 23:19)

The Belt of Truth

Recently, I kept hearing these words, "Put on the *full* armor of God." I went right to Ephesians 6:11 and began to read this very familiar passage again. I read up to verse fourteen where Paul says, "*Stand therefore, having girded your waist with truth*" and it was as if the comma shouted, "Stop!" The Lord showed me it was important to be fully covered. He was emphasizing that *truth* is the first thing we must put on. Everything else comes *afterward*. You may be wondering what this has to do with being transformed by the Word of God. I would like to share the nugget of truth.

Roman soldiers girded themselves with a belt. Straps of leather would hang from this belt providing protection to the lower part of the body (the Nelson Study Bible, p. 1992). Just as this belt of leather protected the soldier, the Lord was saying the belt of truth protects the *vulnerable places* of reproduction (loins) in our lives.

If we are going to stand against the deception and lies of the enemy, we are going to have to be honest in the vulnerable places of our life (in Psalm 51 David said the Lord desired truth in the inward parts).

The enemy does not want transformation. He does not want you to know who you are in Christ. He wants you to believe a lie so he can cheat you out of your destiny. He wants to influence you to receive a hard heart. Solomon declared that we are to keep our heart with all diligence. What flows from our heart, affects every issue in our life (Proverbs 4:23-24). If we do not allow honesty to penetrate our hearts, we will not be fully covered and protected.

Vulnerable places are those areas in our lives that may be wounded or liable to injury. This would indicate sensitive and private areas. I personally believe this especially involves emotions.

The pastor who had invited me to preach my first official sermon hurt me. Although I had experienced an incredible meeting, the ride home was a major battle. The enemy wanted me to focus on the words spoken *to* me rather than those spoken *through* me. The Lord has had to remind me time and time again that I do not wrestle with flesh and blood. The enemy creeps into the places of our hearts where we are easily injured, especially private places of thought where emotions are developed. He slips in with rejection, worry, lust, greed, pride, anger, rebellion, and suspicion. This includes suspicion toward the Lord and others. The heart is where things are reproduced. The enemy tried to get me to reproduce resentment toward that pastor. He rode home on my shoulder that night. He whispered, "Are you going to let him get by with that? He made you feel like a wounded dog. He made you feel like running home with your tail between your legs. Others will think that way too. You might as well quit." I would have too, if it were not for the transforming power of God's Word! His Word and His Spirit rose up in me. This exam came after I had completed my Bible study. It served to approve my faith and to transform my mentality. Without the transforming power of the Word, I would have failed.

Thank God, He always causes us to triumph. By the strength of the Word, I was able to keep my heart right. Transformation took place and I was able to celebrate a magnificent victory.

Truth comes to expose and extract the pain in our lives. If it is not extracted, it will continue to reproduce the same old mess. The Word reveals what is in our hearts so that we will repent. Repentance allows the Lord to usher in healing, release, and change.

Sow Seeds of Transformation

In the Parable of the Sower, Jesus said the seed is the Word of God (Luke 8:11). He directly speaks to the ability to *hear*. Our ability to hear the Word has a lot to do with the condition of our heart. The devil wants to steal the Word from our hearts. Why? If he can steal it, it will not be reproduced.

Adam and Eve were guilty, naked, and afraid when they heard the Lord's voice. They responded to His voice according to the guilty condition of their heart. This caused them to hide from the Lord's presence.

Paul told the church at Colosse to let the Word of Christ dwell richly or abundantly in their hearts (Colossians 3:16). Brief, superficial encounters with the Word of God will not due. Unless the Word is established in our hearts, we will not stand; instead we will fall away in the time of temptation.

If we were to liken the heart to a garden, we would realize that it must be weeded. If the weeds are not pulled out, they will overgrow the good that is planted. The weeds try to grow in the vulnerable places. In Luke 8:14, Jesus especially spoke of worry, greed, and the pleasures of life. These things choke out the Word that has been heard and no fruit is brought to maturity, but the heart that hears the Word, accepts and honors it will be productive. May I plead with you to keep sowing the Word in your heart? What you sow today, you will reap tomorrow. If we want transformation, we must sow the seed of the Word. It is important to take *heed* how we hear.

Making reference again to Paul's words to Timothy, he told him that deception would abound due to evil men and imposters (2 Timothy 3:13). The strategy is found in the words, *"But you must continue in the things which you have learned and been assured of . . . that from childhood you have known the Holy Scriptures"* (2 Timothy 3:14-15). Tending the seeds will keep away the weeds.

> *Yet in all these things we are more than*
> *conquerors through Him who loved us.*
> Romans 8:37

Chapter 9

Born-Again To Overcome

Paul wrote in Romans 6:23, "*the gift of God is eternal life in Christ Jesus our Lord.*" What does eternal life look like? It is an invisible force or power flowing from Jesus affecting our *desires*, *thoughts*, *ideas*, *dreams*, and *urges*.

Jesus had a conversation with a very educated and influential man named Nicodemus, a ruler of the Jews. Jesus spoke to him about being born-again. Without this experience, a person can not see the kingdom of God. Nicodemus tried to understand how this could be possible. Jesus explains it to him in John 3:5-8. From verse eight, we see an illustration of the work of the Holy Spirit in a person's life.

> *The wind blows where it wishes, and*
> *you hear the sound of it, but cannot*
> *tell where it comes from and where it*

> *goes. So is everyone who is born of*
> *the Spirit.*

Just as sin is an invisible force, so is eternal life. You can see the effects of it! You can not see the wind, but you can feel it on your face. We can't see from what direction it comes, but the leaves can be seen waving in the trees. When we are born-again, there is a change. The things you once desired are replaced with new desires. The thoughts you once entertained now embarrass you. The dreams you once dreamed now seem frivolous and selfish. The impulses and urges you once acted on without any thought now carry conviction. You do not see where it comes from, but you know that eternal life is *there*.

The Gift of Eternal Life

After becoming born-again, I had a strong desire to be someone God could use. I would weep in my prayers asking Him to allow me the privilege to influence lives with the eternal life of God. That may seem very strange to you, but it was there. I was surprised by it many times. I was the one who could not speak in front of people, the insecure one, and the one who felt like a failure.

I don't believe it was just *my* desire, but His. I had a desire to know and please God all my life. Due to my identity crisis, emotionally I felt like I was in a tug-of-war. I was caught between two desires; wanting to please God, and wanting Him to lift this crazy notion. After all, it was *impossible* wasn't it? It wasn't lifted though, it remained and grew stronger. I believe the gift of eternal life affected my desires, dreams, and urges. I believe it has affected yours too. I want to encourage you to dare to dream big dreams. In the words of my dad, "Dream big, or stay at home."

Desiring the Anointing

My greatest desire was to walk in a degree of anointing that would convict sinners, heal the sick, and set the captives free. My heartbeat was to be an anointed preacher of the Word. Jesus said He would accompany His Word with signs and wonders. I had watched others on TV. I had witnessed traveling evangelists coming through our area. I had read about the apostles in the book of Acts, but I wanted the anointing to flow from me. How to walk in the anointing was a constant question on my mind. I knew everyone was created in the image of God, created to express an aspect of Himself that no one else could. I knew I was called to preach. I recognized the gifts of the Holy Spirit, and had been used many times, but I wanted to walk in a greater consistency.

God has a plan and purpose for every individual. Jesus came to give us abundant life. The devil comes to steal that life. Let us go back to the garden. The devil understood that Adam and Eve were made in the image and likeness of God. They carried in them the life of God. They enjoyed intimate fellowship. In the same way the enemy affected Adam and Eve's relationship, he tries to affect ours. He wants that flow of life to be broken. Once broken, he counts on paralysis to keep us from fulfilling our destiny.

Earlier, it was stated that Jesus, once He completed His work on the cross, became qualified to offer eternal life. There is a lesson here for all of us. Jesus gained authority by the things He obediently suffered. Paul was given authority by going through some very trying difficulties. I am convinced we are entrusted with authority only *after* going through some things as well.

Hard Victories

When my son, Tony, was about eight years old, he woke up one night from a bad dream. I did not know it would be the beginning of one of the longest trials of my life. For the next three years, I would have to deal with a demonic spirit of fear. It tormented him day and night. I felt so powerless. At other times, I would be filled with anger. This precious child was being robbed of peace, sleep, and normalcy. I did not know what to do. I had him prayed for by every anointed person I knew. I prayed. I fasted. I bound. I loosed. I believed God. I quoted scriptures. At times, I even cried. "Lord, why don't I have an answer?"

It is not my desire to hurt or embarrass my son. This was not his fault. It was a spiritual battle. It is shared for the purpose of explaining the turn around in the level of anointing I was walking in. It is a part of the answer to my prayer, "Anoint me and then use me, Lord." This evil spirit of fear would mostly manifest at night. Bed time would come, and I would bless and pray for my son. I would try to leave the room, but his eyes would be filled with terror. There were so many nights I would sing in the Spirit to get him to go to sleep. It seemed to have a soothing effect on him. When I would think he was asleep, I would get up to leave, and he would be wide awake again. Sometimes, it would take hours before I could leave him alone in his room for the night.

There were times he would seem like things were alright. He could be in the house alone. He would play outside with his little sister Cheryl. Then other times, he would leap from an entire flight of stairs. Once he jumped on my back terrified and filled with fear. During this time, I was pregnant with my third child, Elisha. One night I had gone to the bathroom in the dark, tripped over my son's mini trampoline and fell. He heard me hit the floor with a thud and a groan and ran to help me, terrified that something bad had happened. He lived in continual fear. It was a very difficult thing to walk through and I couldn't seem to get the victory. He was just a little boy and he did not deserve this. It was hard to understand when I could not see or hear what he seen and heard. I began to ask the Lord to let it manifest because I did not know what I was dealing with.

We would discover that he had watched a vampire movie at his then unsaved grandfather's house. Watching this movie opened a door to fear. Not only had he watched the movie, but just months before he had lost his paternal grandfather. They were very close. My son was very sorry for watching the movie. He had been put to bed on a pallet on the floor while his grandfather was watching the movie. It wasn't until he was engrossed in the movie that he realized what it was about. By then, he was too scared to leave the room.

One particular summer night, I had stayed up late to talk to my husband on the phone because he was out of town. I was completely exhausted. I remember silently asking the Lord to let it be a good night. I had experienced so many sleepless nights. I just wanted to go to sleep. As I placed my foot on the last step leading to our upstairs, I was well aware of *that* presence. I went to bed hoping it would go away. Not long after falling asleep, I sensed someone watching me. I opened my eyes and saw my son standing in the doorway of my bedroom, but . . . there was someone else standing with him. I sat up in bed. My first reaction was it is his dad. By this time I was wide awake and realized it was not his dad, I had just spoken to him on the phone earlier that night.

What I saw was the form of a man. It did not have a face. It did seem to have a distinct gray outline. On top of its head were ears like those of a cat. Its hand seemed to be holding my sons elbow. I was scared. I was angry and I was unsure what to do. So I prayed. Authority rose up in me. Revelation came to my mind. I told that thing to let go of my son in the name of Jesus! When I spoke, my son ran to my bed and hid himself in the covers. The Lord showed me how this spirit thought it was my sons "pet." I addressed that as well. I set the record straight and declared that it had no rights to my son. He did not belong to this spirit but to the Lord Jesus Christ. I then commanded it to leave. The next part puzzles me to this day.

This evil spirit left my doorway and slipped behind the linen closet door. It had been left open about six inches. I could see the gray outline of fingers holding onto the door peeking out at me. I further questioned the Lord. "What am I supposed to do now? I told it to go in Your name. I thought demons were subject to Your name?" The only answer He gave me that night was a statement: "Look inside you." I knew what He meant. He was telling me to take my focus off the spirit and place my attention on the fact that the greater One lived in me. My response to the Lord was, "How am I supposed to do that with that *thing* standing there?" His reply was, "Worship Me." I began to lift up my voice in praise and worship. I started to bless the Lord and sing love songs to Him. The peaceful presence of the Lord filled that room and we both slipped off to sleep.

It had been revealed. I had seen what my son was aware of. My heart melted with such compassion. Guilt filled my heart because of the times I was not as sympathetic as I should have been. My child had been suffering in silence.

Years passed and we even moved into another house. The intensity of the attacks did diminish, but freedom had not been realized.

My son was now 11. One night he came and stood by my bed. I asked, "Are you feeling afraid?" He nodded his head yes. I invited him to get in bed with me. We began to talk. He began to speak about his paternal grandfather's death as if it had happened the day before. During that conversation, the Lord finally revealed to me that a fear of death and dying had taken hold of my son. I turned on the light and opened up the Bible and took him to Job. I explained how the Lord had a hedge around Job and that God had one around him too.

Something happened that night. The enemy had been exposed. Victory began. The darkness was lifted and light began to shine. You could literally feel it in the atmosphere. Hallelujah! May God get the glory! You may be reading this and having trouble believing my story. I had second thoughts about sharing it, but felt released by the Lord to go ahead. It is not my intention to imply that everyone has to go through a similar experience to have authority, but I do want to convey there is a cost. There are some things to go through, learn from, and walk out.

The Anointing Is the Holy Ghost

Then some of the itinerant Jewish exorcists took it upon themselves to call the name of the Lord Jesus over those who had evil spirits, saying, "We exorcise you by the Jesus whom Paul preaches." Also there were seven sons of Sceva, a Jewish chief priest, who did so. And the evil spirit answered and said, "Jesus I know, and Paul I know; but who are you?" Then the man in whom the evil spirit was leaped on them, overpowered

> *them and prevailed against them, so*
> *that they fled out of that house naked*
> *and wounded.*
> (Acts 19:13-16)

This passage of Scripture has so much to say to us. First of all, I do not believe we are to just take things upon ourselves. These men were mimicking Jesus and Paul without wisdom or any personal knowledge of their own. The idea was, "If Jesus and Paul can do it, then we can do it too." Their focus was completely wrong. It wasn't about them; it was about the man in whom the evil spirit was living.

Jesus did not begin to walk in the power of the anointing as soon as He left His mother's womb. He was a grown man. The Bible tells us He grew and became strong, being filled with wisdom, and having the grace of God upon Him (Luke 2:40). He increased in wisdom and stature, and in favor with God and man (Luke 2:52).

We also know, according to the book of Galatians, that Paul grew and increased in the school of the Spirit before he ever saw a dark mist fall on a sorcerer and blind him (Acts 13:11). There was a growing time before God worked unusual miracles by his hands (Acts 19:11).

From my own experience, I know we don't walk in power, anointing, and authority over-night either. We develop and increase as we have relationship with the Lord Jesus. We get to know Him intimately. Trust is gained. Understanding comes. Faith grows. Purpose is revealed, and an awareness of Who lives in us and why He lives in us is realized. In Acts 10:38 we read, *"How God anointed Jesus of Nazareth with the Holy Spirit and with power, who went about doing good and healing all who were oppressed by the devil, for God was with Him."* The anointing is the Holy Ghost! It isn't how much we pray or fast. It is not where we go to church. It is not how we were raised (although these are important factors). It is not about being educated. It is not based on how much we have failed. It *is* the person and power of the Holy Spirit.

The things mentioned above can hinder the Holy Spirit but they are not who the Holy Spirit is nor are they His anointing.

My ministry really began to change when I saw Who lived in me and why. He wanted to flow from me to touch humanity. He wanted to reveal Himself to lost and hurting people. He wanted to prove His Word. Again, it was not about my past, it was about their future. It was not about my failure, but His success.

We have the anointing because the Anointed One lives in us!

The Glory Brings Anointing

In chapter six, we saw how the Lord wants us to reflect His glory. Paul showed us from 2 Corinthians 3:18 that when we behold the glory of the Lord, we are transformed by the Holy Spirit.

This word glory as already mentioned has a very unusual meaning. If I were to ask you to define the word glory, what would you say? Many say it is the presence of God and this is true. However, according to The New Strong's Expanded Exhaustive Concordance (p.70), the word glory means "an ever-growing opinion, and honor that results from that opinion." Again, this describes intimacy.

As we see the glory of the Lord, our opinion of who He is changes. We see Him as He really is, not who we thought Him to be. In Isaiah six, Isaiah said, "*I see the Lord high and lifted up!*" His opinion changed. We have to understand that he was in the midst of wickedness. I am sure he was distracted by it, but when he saw the holiness of God, he realized his sinfulness (verse five). Repentance took place in his heart and immediately the Lord touched his mouth with a coal of fire taken from the altar.

Being in the presence of God brought focus. It brought a renewed opinion that God was holy. From this changed opinion, he was made pure for serving the true King. After Isaiah's cleansing, he was put into ministry. He was eager, "Here I am Lord, please send me!" The glory (having a right opinion) of the Lord was key to his anointing. The anointing was given to him in order to speak to unclean people.

We just said that the anointing is the Holy Spirit. We can then say the Holy Spirit is the glory of the Lord. Jesus said it like this in John 16:14, "*He will glorify Me, for He will take of what is Mine and declare it to you.*" The Holy Spirit will make Jesus known to us. He will reveal truth to us, and He will bring us the anointing. The Holy Spirit anointed Isaiah, and from that point on, his words became light and power to those who heard him. Sin convinces us to blend in, but God desires for us to stand out! Jesus said we were to be a light to the world. As a light, we illuminate the way for others to see the glory of the Lord, and have their opinion of Him change also. They, like Isaiah, will worship Him. This is what the Lord Jesus wants, all men everywhere to be saved.

The Anointing Is Life

Again, the anointing is the Holy Ghost. In John 6:63, Jesus said it is the Spirit who gives life. Paul testified of this life living in him.

> *I have been crucified with Christ; it is no longer I who live, but Christ lives in me; and the life which I now live in the flesh I live by faith in the Son of God, who loved me and gave Himself for me.*
>
> (Galatians 2:20)

Jesus was living in Paul. The Holy Spirit is at work in the life of the one who puts his faith in Jesus. We have been born-again and given power to overcome everything thrown at us, so that the purposes of God may be fulfilled. His purposes are His desires in us. He then empowers us with the Holy Spirit, the anointing, to accomplish the work He has given us to do.

In Ephesians 2:8, Paul writes, "*For by grace you have been saved through faith, and that not of yourselves; it is the gift of God.*" Verse ten gives us the reason, "*For we are His workmanship, created in Christ Jesus for good works, which God prepared beforehand that we should walk in them.*"

The Holy Spirit is life, eternal life, the kind of life Paul was speaking about. The Holy Spirit is instrumental in helping us to understand the good works that have been prepared for us. Because we now have life by faith in the One who lives in us, it is vital that we live for Him. This new life, this invisible force, allows us to be sensitive to the desires of God's heart. For me, I strongly wanted to see sinners be convicted by the drawing power of the Holy Spirit. I had seen myself standing before multitudes of people. I wanted to walk in the anointing that healed broken hearts and bodies. For years, I thought I had to apologize for this desire, but now I realize it was not mine, it was His. It was my calling. I believe the Lord wants everyone to know why He has created them. I would challenge you to pursue the heartbeat of God for your life. Remember, He is not hiding it from you. He is keeping it for you. It's so amazing how the life of God brings personal life, and through you brings life to others. This is only possible by the work and anointing of the Holy Spirit.

Anointed To Serve

It should be obvious by now that God wants us to see people the way He sees them. If we are going to see others, we can not be looking at ourselves. The anointing, the call, the gifts, the desires, it is all for others. Jesus loves people. People are His passion.

People do not realize how valuable they are. Our job as children of God is to help them realize their value. Remember, when it came to creation, God was only personally involved when He created man. Everything else was spoken into existence, but He formed man Himself.

Several years ago, I was sent an email telling a story about a twenty dollar bill. I have used it many times, especially in foreign lands. Although I do not know who the author is, I would like to say they deserve the credit. I may not get the whole story right, but this is how I have used it. I would take out a bill; the amount depended on where I was. In Africa, an American twenty dollar bill is a lot of money. In America, I may have to use a hundred dollar bill. While holding it up, I would ask people what it was, an obvious answer. Many at this point would say, "I'll take it, may I have it?"

After verifying its worth, I would take it and crumble it up the best I could. Then I would throw it on the ground and stomp all over it. If I were outdoors in Africa, that old red clay would have it looking a mess. If I were in Jamaica, it would be grass stained, and full of holes from where the rocks had poked through. If I were in a building, it would usually rip or tear. People are usually astonished at this point. What was within reach and valuable, was now a torn, dirty, and crumbled up mess. As I lift it up again before the people, I share with them that this bill is a lot like many of them. They have been crumbled and bruised by life. Many of them have been stained by sin and made dirty. Others have been ripped in two by sin or perhaps circumstances they could not control. Here is the good part . . . it is *still* a twenty dollar bill! It is *still* a hundred dollar bill! Although it has been worn, torn, and made dirty, it is still worth twenty dollars. It is still worth a hundred dollars. I could take it to any bank, exchange it, and receive its value.

Right about now, the tears would be flowing down people's cheeks. People have been made in the image and likeness of God. When I find myself getting really aggravated with someone, the Lord will remind me of their value.

How will people know this unless you and I tell them? All of us have been called to go into the world and tell others about Jesus and His gift of life. They cannot hear unless we speak up. Do not remain silent! I hear some of you right now thinking, "You don't know what I have done in the past. You don't know what I have been through. You don't understand the injustice I have suffered." Excuses! They are all excuses. That's what mine were; high school drop out, pregnant teenage statistic, a failure. Please do not misunderstand me, I care about what you have been through, but Jesus is greater than your past. He is mightier than your pain. He suffered unjustly for your injustice.

Your past, your pain, and your injustice qualify you to speak. Your life, like the dollar bill, was marred and ugly, but Jesus died for you anyway. You and I can relate to others because we were crumbled, dirty, and torn lives that Jesus has redeemed.

> *A word fitly spoken is like apples of*
> *gold in settings of silver.*
> (Proverbs 25:11)

This verse describes the value of the words we speak. They are valuable messages to valuable people. The importance is the gospel message, not the messenger of the gospel. The message of the Gospel is alive and full of power.

A New Level

Now that my desire for wanting the anointing has been explained, I would like to share a pivotal turning point. Just as Isaiah had his coal from the altar experience, I had mine.

Quite a few years ago, I was to attend a prayer and fasting conference. To tell you the truth, if money were not involved, I would not have gone. I had a bad attitude. Nothing seemed to be going right. I was frustrated with my ministry. I was disgusted with so many different things, but honestly I can not remember a single one.

This conference was scheduled to start on Friday and go the whole weekend. I had to preach at a particular church the next night, so I only went for the one night. I was not prepared for what would take place.

I was sitting with a few ladies from my church. We were in the middle of the worship service and all I could think about was food. I was so sorry it was a fasting conference. I was distracted by the meeting I was to do the next night, wondering what to preach.

I really just did not want to be there. In the midst of all these thoughts, I prayed and asked God to help me. Within minutes, I felt this warm light shining on me. It seemed like a small spot light. I opened my eyes but nothing was there. It felt pretty good. All of a sudden, I could focus. My mind was upon the Lord. I began to sing. Shortly after that, the whole group began to sing in the Spirit. The presence of the Lord was filling the place. At least, it was filling my space. The next thing I knew, I was singing in the Spirit, but it was not my normal voice. It sounded angelic. It flowed from me in a very specific pattern not known to me. It startled me. I questioned the Lord and He spoke to me that it was Him. He comforted me to trust Him. It is now flowing more freely and getting louder. It was growing. It was coming with more intensity. I decided to yield to it. After all, the Lord told me it was Him. As this angelic pattern, a language in song, streamed from within me, my hand began to move in a circular motion. It just seemed like me and Jesus, yet my mind raced with thoughts of what people might think. That was my problem, wasn't it? I was always thinking about me.

By this time, I was slightly bent forward at the waist, one foot in front of the other. My arm was still moving in circles and this heavenly song was singing out from deep within me. I asked the Lord about all that was happening. He told me I was interceding for people I had not yet ministered to. The circular motion of my arm was representing the world. I began to weep. It was so glorious. I was so unworthy. I had come with a bad attitude, now the glory of God was upon me. Thank God for His mercy and His grace. I learned it wasn't about me; it was about His purpose in me.

Believe me, the next thing that happened, ministered to me more than anything. Do you remember my struggle with the fear, "What if I don't have enough stuff?" It would find an answer that night. One I have never forgotten, one that changed the course of my life and ministry. I felt fingers on both sides of my mouth pulling and stretching my lips. "Okay Lord, now I am sure that this looks ridiculous." In my mind, I was sure that everyone could see what I was feeling. My mouth felt distorted. It felt drawn and stretched. Isaiah had a coal of fire; I got the fingers of God. It was interesting to me, that after Isaiah had the coal touch his lips, the Lord gave him direction. The words I heard the Lord speak to me that night were similar to Isaiah. He was sending me too. He said, "*I am opening wide your mouth, and I will fill it.*"

I would find out later, this experience lasted around forty minutes. When it lifted, I felt like a wet noodle. I went back to my hotel room and rested in the Lord, pondering all that had happened to me. The evidence that something significant had happened manifested the next night where I was preaching. The anointing to preach was stronger. There was more conviction, more power. My sensitivity to the voice of the Holy Spirit appeared to be more keen, more sure, and accurate. I knew I had stepped into a new dimension. Thank you Lord!

Anxiety had been a part of my life. As much as I wanted to preach, when an invitation would come,

I would almost panic. "What do I say, Lord." I was fearful that I would make a fool of myself. After this experience, anxiety began to lesson, and a wonderful confidence began to rise up in me. Much later, I came across Acts 13:2. It was as if the Lord was explaining what happened to me. It was validated.

> *As they ministered to the Lord and fasted, the Holy Spirit said, "Now separate to Me Barnabas and Saul for the work to which I have called them."*

Saul and Barnabas had been anointed. They were called before this but they had been doing other things, but this was a special affirmation for a new phase of ministry. Because the Holy Spirit was sending them (v. 4), a new level of power was now following them.

Even King David was called to be a king, long before he became the king. There was a waiting time, but it was fulfilled. The moment came when it was the right time to step up and be the ruler. You will come into your appointed time too. God is faithful. His ways are higher than our ways. There is a reward to the hardships we overcome.

A New Devil

A couple of years had passed since my mouth had been stretched. I was thankful for this new dimension of the anointing in my life and ministry. However, I was developing a yearning to see more people healed. I read every book by or about Kathryn Kuhlman. Fifteen years earlier, it had been prophesied that I would have a similar ministry. Once again, the word came, the call was revealed, but it would be years before I would walk in any degree of the anointing as she did.

Around this time, a phone call came from a pastor in another state. He was looking for a woman evangelist to come and minister at his church. He asked me a few questions and we spoke for a few minutes. One question in particular had something to do with my explanation of why I should be the one to come to his church to minister. I was honest with him. From my heart, I shared how I did not just want another meeting invitation; I wanted the presence of the Lord. He became very quiet. I thought to myself, "You have blown this chance." He finally replied back and said, "I think you might be exactly what we are looking for." We booked a meeting to take place a few weeks later. I was so excited. God had been doing some awesome things. He was opening more doors. Still, I was not seeing the manifestation of the Holy Spirit like I wanted. I was getting ready to; I just didn't know it.

After arriving, I met the elderly lady I was to stay with. She shared with me that she saw a glow of fire around me. She also sensed that I was feeling frustrated because I was not shooting as straight as I wanted. Like the rings that circle the planet Saturn, she saw rings around me. It appeared to her that I was off balance. What she didn't know was that prior to leaving home, I had a vision of spirits flying around my head. It concerned me so I inquired of the Lord to see if I should stay in a hotel by myself. His answer, "Don't think you will waltz up there without any opposition." Once again, I felt as if the Lord had left me hanging.

The Lord had also given me a dream before I left. In the dream, a mafia man was flattering me. He wanted to know everything about me. Sensing him to be evil and controlling, I left. When I woke up, I had this inkling that I should not underestimate the enemy. The very first night of the week long meeting, I was approached by a man. He looked a lot like the man in my dream. He would stay after service and talk with me. He expressed flattering words to me. He shared how he recognized my calling and the gifts in my life.

God was doing incredible things in the meetings. People were being touched by the power of God. People were being healed. What I had longed for was happening in a greater degree. There was a man who had torn ligaments in his arm. He came for prayer and at first there was no change. I spoke with a confidence that came from the Lord, if Jesus prayed twice, perhaps we should pray again. We prayed once more and he began to twist his arm to the right and then to the left. He told me that he was not able to do that before. God had done something doctors could not do.

There were other testimonies of healing too. A young high school student was not able to make basketball practice due to an injury. I kicked him under the anointing, and he went to basketball practice the very next day.

I share these things because there was also something else going on behind the scenes. At night, when I would go back to my room, I could not sleep. Each night, the attack was more severe. I had not spoken of it to anyone. Driving home on Thursday night, I shared with the lady I was staying with what was happening at night. I also told her about the vision I had about the spirits flying around my head. She also relayed an experience she had in intercession for me before I arrived. At first she was offended that it might be something in her house, but later that night, the Lord would use her. By this time in the week, I was experiencing a lot of nausea. Even during worship that night, I had to sit down because I felt so weak. I sat there praying for deliverance, but it did not come. I did not understand how the Lord could be touching all those people through me and yet bypass me!

I had only about ten hours sleep since I had arrived Saturday night. I had never experienced insomnia until that week. This particular Thursday night, I thought I would sleep because I was so exhausted. The moment I lay my head on the pillow, I was aware of that presence I had known many times before. Believe me, it was not holy either. Tears are streaming down my face. I do not know what to do. Again I bound everything I knew to bind. I loosed the supernatural ability of God to bring me sleep, but nothing happened, nothing changed. It was about three in the morning so I prayed and asked the Lord to put me on someone's heart so that they might pray for me. I did sense a bit of peace, but still sleep did not come.

The next morning, I got up to use the bathroom. The lady called me from her room. When she spoke my name, the hair rose up on my arms. I went into her room and she sheepishly said to me, "It is in my house." I was not sure what she was talking about. She said, "The spirit from your dream, it is here." She further explained to me how she awoke around three in the morning. She had my attention. She went on to tell me how she saw a cat go into my room. You have to understand she saw this by the Holy Spirit. My door was closed. She then watched the cat vomit next to my bed. Afterward, she heard it speak these words, "I am going to kill the messenger." I would like to tell you that my response was one of concern, but it was really one of stupidity. I chimed back with great confidence that he was unable to kill me. It would be years later before I would again remember these words.

Later that morning, I did call an evangelist friend of mine to ask for prayer. He quoted these words to me, "A new level a new devil." In his opinion, because I was carrying a new anointing the enemy was attacking me. He also felt as if I were dealing with witchcraft. I knew I was dealing with something I had not dealt with before. When I asked his opinion about the man in the meetings who resembled the mafia, he said there was a spirit operating through him trying to court me. The jest of it being, the devil was after the life of God flowing from me. No wonder Jesus left us this information in John 10:10,

"The thief does not come except to steal, and to kill, and to destroy."

He was stealing my sleep and now he wanted to steal the life of God, the anointing flowing from me? Why? Didn't he know that I was just a housewife from Indiana? I realized the incredible value that resided inside of me. As Paul said, "We have this treasure in earthen vessels. It is the power of God." It is amazing how the devil has more revelation of the power of God than we do.

I would like to tell you that things changed after the Lord revealed all of this to me. I continued to battle fatigue until I left on Saturday. Even after returning home, I felt a great sense of weariness. A couple of weeks later, I spoke with a sister in the Lord. She told me how she had a similar experience. She felt as if the spirit operating in this man was still pulling on me, still thinking of me. It did eventually subside.

I am not saying I understand everything that happened, but I did learn a great lesson. The Lord showed me that the enemy had strategies to hinder the flow of the anointing in our lives. We have power over all the works of the enemy. The Lord did bring me through, and once again something was added to me.

The enemy is always plotting to stop the work of God.

One word of advice, guard the life of God in you. Guard it with everything you have. It is so precious. It is so valuable the thief wants it. If he can't steal it, he will try to stop it by bringing difficulties into your life. You must push through them. You must recognize that the very life he is trying to steal is the source of your deliverance.

Suffering Is not a Bad Word

Please understand my only reason for sharing these life lessons is to let you know the knowledge I have obtained by going through them. Knowledge I probably could not have gained any other way. Believe me there is more I don't understand than I do understand, but one thing is certain, the knowledge I do have came *afterward*.

May I remind you of Paul's words concerning the life of Jesus Christ?

> *But what things were gain to me, these I have counted loss for Christ. Yet indeed I also count all things loss for the excellence of the knowledge of Christ Jesus my Lord, for whom I have suffered the loss of all things, and count them as rubbish, that I may gain Christ and be found in Him, not having my own righteousness, which is from the law, but that which is through faith in Christ, the righteousness which is from God by faith; that I may know Him and the power of His resurrection, and the fellowship of His sufferings, being conformed to His*

> *death, if by any means, I may attain to*
> *the resurrection from the dead.*
> (Philippians 3:7-11)

The value of knowing Christ was better than anything else he had known or experienced. Being a Jew and following all the rules and regulations used to identify Paul, but now he drew his identity from knowing Christ. He too, had an afterward understanding of things. He considered life before Christ as rubbish, meaning worthless and detestable. Life now was Christ Jesus Himself!

Paul became intimately acquainted with Him through his daily relationship. It wasn't just head knowledge it was revelation in his heart. It was also something he continued to experience. It was Paul's choice and desire to know Jesus through every experience of life. Whether it was the ongoing ministry of power he received regularly (the gifts, direction, or strength by the Holy Spirit) or the times he suffered (shipwrecks, beatings, and prison), it really didn't matter. He wanted to know Him. New life in Christ was his choice. A choice he never regretted. A choice he protected and cherished.

Paul went through things he probably would not have gone through as a Hebrew. He experienced hardships because he was identified with Christ. More importantly, he attained knowledge of Jesus; knowledge he could not have received any other way than through the things he suffered. We, too, will go through things, but the good news is we will get through them! We hold on to Jesus differently in times of suffering than we do in times of victory. We desperately draw near to Him and lovingly depend on Him when there is no human way out. In these intimate times, we really do get to know Him.

*But the manifestation of the Spirit is given to
each one for the profit of all.*
1 Corinthians 12:7

Chapter 10

Born-Again To Accomplish

During Jesus' earthly ministry, He endured trials. He was persecuted, scorned, and mocked. He even had His deeds credited to the devil. At the end of it all, it was still His desire to please His Father. He was driven to fulfill His intended purpose for the sake of humanity. It was all for the joy of future people being saved (Hebrews 12:2). His attention was not on the cross, but on the reward the cross would bring!

It is the Lord's desire that you and I finish the work that He has planned for us. May we also, after all the trials, be found with the same passion to finish our course? I used to think it wasn't that big of a deal. Sure I knew the Lord had something for each of us to do. Why was it so important? It is because lives depend on it.

In John 4, Jesus had been holding a conversation with a woman He met at a well. The disciples had gone to the grocery store, and when they returned they found Jesus talking with this woman. No one was willing to ask any questions. Curiosity would have compelled me to ask. Instead, they tried to get Jesus to eat. Jesus used it as an opportunity to teach His followers a very important lesson. He responds to their carnality with spirituality. Notice His comment, *"I have food to eat of which you do not know"* (John 4:32). I can hear the disciples, can't you? "Excuse me we just walked into town to buy food. Why would you make us do that if you already had food?" The next verse suggests that they were thinking someone might have already fed Him. They were always a little slow when Jesus was trying to make a point. *"My food is to do the will of Him who sent Me, and to finish His work"* (John 4:34). Something was sustaining Him other than a steak and baked potato. It wasn't enough to know His Father's will; He had to completely finish it. Strength was released to Him when He chose to please His Father.

I see several truths that can be applied to our walk with the Lord. First of all, God wants us to be productive. Jesus is our example. He had a purpose and nothing was going to distract Him from that purpose, especially a meal. While they were buying food, He was working. He was accomplishing His Father's will. Secondly, it appears from the next verse, that Jesus is offering them an opportunity to get involved. *"Do you not say, 'There are still four months and then comes the harvest?' Behold I say to you, lift up your eyes and look at the fields, for they are already white for harvest!"* (John 4:35). He wanted them to know the joy, to experience the satisfaction that came from working for the Father. I believe He wants that for us too.

It is my personal conviction that Jesus is still trying to get His followers to understand and appreciate the fulfillment that comes from being an active participant in the work of the kingdom. He is still trying to instill a work ethic. We, many times, would also rather recline at the table of comfort than be busy working for our master. Jesus was always trying to move the disciples forward. You and I have been given the gift of salvation for the purpose of finishing His intended work for us. It is not enough to know that you have a work to do, it is crucial that you accomplish it. Jesus is glorified and people are saved and benefit.

He Is a Rewarder

> *But without faith it is impossible to please Him, for he who comes to God must believe that He is, and that He is a rewarder of those who diligently seek Him.*
>
> (Hebrews 11:6)

We have established that God has a plan for every individual. We have discovered His reason for saving us is the works He has prepared for us (Ephesians 2:10). We have been promised help and know how through the blessing of the Holy Spirit. We witnessed Jesus inviting His disciples to follow His example and work in the kingdom. All these things must be real-ized as we approach Him. We need to understand He is everything He says and so much more. Faith is necessary to please the Lord. Jesus pleased the Father because He trusted and obeyed Him. I do not think Jesus would have went to the cross had He not been able to trust His Father.

Trusting Jesus is how we please Him. When He tells you He has use of you and wants you to preach His Word, and you pursue that with complete trust, He is pleased. When He tells you to give a thousand dollars, and you obey without question, He is pleased. Serving Him is filled with promise and surprise because He is always a step ahead of you. Seeking to please Him brings reward. Although we experience some of the reward here, much of it will be celebrated on the other side. Listen to the promise of Jesus in Revelation 22:12, *"And behold, I am coming quickly, and My reward is with Me, to give to everyone according to his work."* Knowing that Jesus will reward those who accomplish their work is what motivates me. Remember, Jesus was rewarded the privilege to sit at His Father's right hand after He finished His work on the cross.

I have to say it again, Jesus Himself is our *reward*!

This brings to mind something else the Lord revealed to me. I just have to share it with you. It will enlarge your perception of Him.

He Gives a Guarantee

You know the Lord is for you, don't you? Believe me; He is in your corner. He is fighting for you, but He is also cheering for you. He wants you to make it. Because He continues forever, He is able to save you wholly and completely.

> *Therefore He is also able to save to the uttermost those who come to God through Him, since He always lives to make intercession for them.*
> (Hebrews 7:25)

As our High Priest, He made an oath, a promise, or a guarantee (Hebrews 7:20). His office as High Priest will never expire! It will continue always and forever. He is able to save us as long as you and I continue to come to Him. It is ongoing and constant. The Holy Spirit is always at work in us sanctifying and making us holy. Did you get the other part of His promise? He is constantly praying for you and me. Jesus' prayers get answered. Jesus is representing you in heaven. What a tremendous relief. There is someone who will never give up on you. He is your defender. How awesome is that?

Wait. There is more. In Hebrews 6:18, we have the guarantee that Jesus can never lie. It is impossible. This is the foundation on which we can base everything! This gives us consolation, encouragement, and peace. He will fulfill all His promises.

He promised He would come for us. In Colossians 1:5, Paul informs us that this hope of His return is laid up in heaven. The author of Hebrews shares another nugget of truth from 6:19-20.

> *This hope we have as an anchor of the soul, both sure and steadfast, and which enters the Presence behind the veil, where the forerunner has entered for us, even Jesus, having become High Priest forever according to the order of Melchizedek.*

Our hope in Jesus Christ is secure! It is likened to an anchor. This truth, this promise guarantees to bring stability to our *souls*. Our emotions do not have to be tossed on waves of uncertainty. Our minds do not have to capsize in the midst of a storm. The storm is only temporary, but heaven is eternal. Our will can be tamed with trust, enabling us to step out of the boat with confidence and assurance. Why? Because this anchor is not embedded in sand, but in the very presence of Almighty God! Oh, I feel a shout coming on right now. Glory to God!

The *forerunner* was a small boat sent out into the harbor to assist larger ships who were unable to enter due to bad weather or damage. This forerunner would take the anchor and drop it inside the harbor securing the larger ship. The word forerunner implies that later on, the larger ship will come into the harbor (The Nelson Study Bible, p. 2085). Are you starting to see the application? Jesus is not only our anchor,

He is our Forerunner. He has taken our anchor and placed it inside heaven and secured it there. Just as the vessel will come into port, we will come into heaven. We can come in like an undamaged ship or a tattered and worn fishing boat. He is ever pulling you and me to safety. He will never pull up the anchor. It will remain fastened there in His presence. We must never abandon ship! If you abandon the ship, you will not finish your course. In Hebrews 12:1, we are exhorted to throw off the excess weight and cargo of our lives and remain on course.

He who finishes wins!

Learning to Yield

Part of accomplishing God's will, is to know what He wants you to do. Accomplishment is a life-long process. I believe there are always new discoveries to make. I like to call them stepping stones. There are things we go through that develop our character, the process of producing fruit.

> *In this you greatly rejoice, though now for a little while, if need be, you have been grieved by various trials, that the genuineness of your faith, being much more precious than gold that perishes, though it is tested by fire, may be found to praise, honor, and glory at the revelation of Jesus Christ.*
>
> (1 Peter 1:6-7)

When we go through things, we call them tests. They are not intended to fail us, but rather to *approve* us. This word was used for coins that were genuine and not debased. The aim is not to destroy but to purify and refine (The Nelson Study Bible, p. 2104). Why? The purpose is one of maturity and usefulness to God.

Following many years of tested faith (James 1:3-4); the Lord was perfecting me so that I might have some endurance. He was consistently working out my defects to bring me to a place where I would be more complete. The Lord was teaching me about yielding to Him. At the prayer and fasting conference, the Lord came to me, but I had to yield to Him. Had I refused to yield, the experience may have passed me by. Although I had some idea of what it meant to yield to the Lord, I sensed He was trying to reveal something more.

More than ten years ago, I began to travel annually to Jamaica. The pastor is one of my dearest friends. They have yield signs just as we do. They are red and shaped like a triangle. Instead of the word yield, they say "give way." What a definition of yielding to the Holy Ghost. "Teach me how to give way to You Lord," was my plea. One particular year, while ministering in Jamaica, the Lord moved on me in the most unusual way. I had been teaching on losing self-consciousness (like chapter three). I was also asking the Lord to show me what He wanted me to understand about yielding to Him.

It was Friday night. I was there with another minister. He would preach three nights and I would preach three nights. For years he would speak to me about tag-team preaching. His father was a minister, and he had seen it many times before in his life. I had never seen it. I was not even sure what it would look like. It was my turn to preach. During worship, the Lord spoke to my heart to kneel while I was on the platform. I argued with Him a little bit because I did not want to draw attention to myself. He told me there were two reasons. The first, He said was to demonstrate another aspect of worship before the people. The second reason, He was asking me to yield to Him. As I knelt, I got caught up in the Spirit. I was praying in the Holy Ghost and my body began to shake, especially my legs. The glory came down that night. The worship leader was truly being used to usher in the presence of the Lord. I did not understand all that was happening to me, but I knew it was the anointing, the Holy Ghost.

Sometime later, I heard the Lord say, "When the pastor gives you the microphone, give it to the other brother." What? You have to be mistaken. The anointing is on *me*. The Lord had spoken. I heard it and I knew it. I was a wee bit agitated about it, but I did obey the Lord. When I handed that microphone to the other brother, he came off that platform like a rocket. It just seemed he was bottled up and ready to explode and he did too. For the next twenty or thirty minutes, he began to prophesy. I stood by the pulpit, my legs still shaking. I did not get it. I had the Holy Ghost on me too. Well, once again, I found myself unprepared for what would happen next. This brother hands me the microphone and says,

"Prophesy." Uummm. Duhhh. What? I do not know how. It was not like I could ask everyone to turn to Hebrews chapter 12. I just did what I knew to do and that was pray in tongues. A few minutes later, he took the microphone from me and started going again. I just stood there feeling a bit stupid. I prayed, "Lord, I do not know what You are doing, but I do not want it to pass me by." My mind was just racing with so many thoughts. I felt confused and a lot of pressure.

As I stood still in the presence of the Lord, I began to feel like the invisible woman. It was as if parts of me were disappearing. I was only conscious of my mouth (there was an emphasis again) and my belly. I could not sense nor feel any other part of my body. The Lord whispered in my ear, "This is yielding." How many moments passed during this time, I was unsure. The next time the brother came to me with that microphone, I preached by the inspiration of the Holy Ghost like never before. It was not me. I could not tell you what I said. It was as if the Lord was bypassing me, and speaking Himself! Glory! For the next fifteen to twenty minutes, I spoke from my spirit in rhyme. I had never done that before. I had not even desired to do that, but I did. I then handed the microphone back to the brother and away he went. The next thing I know, he is handing me the microphone again, and I began to give an altar call.

The anointing was pouring down on the service as if someone were holding buckets of warm honey over our heads. The glory of God was present. It was like the Lord was waving His hands over head, and people were falling by the dozens. I was so inebriated; I needed help to stand up. By the way, as the altar call began, I turned to the brother to see if he wanted to handle it. His reply was, "No, the anointing is on you." The Lord had not forgotten to use me. He was anointing me with a fresh endowment that evidently was directly linked to this new ability to yield. One more thing, this was the closest I had ever come to tag-team preaching. To the Holy Spirit I say, "Tag, You are it!"

The Anointing: Ability to Yield

I discovered a truth that night. For years I had prayed, "Anoint me Lord. I want more anointing. Please give me a double portion of the anointing." I realized the Holy Spirit was more than enough anointing. He *is* the anointing. The key was in my ability to get out of His way and allow Him to flow through me. That was one of the most awesome experiences I ever had. The intention though, was that it be more than an experience, it was to bring me to a place of wholeness. By wholeness, I mean, having reached an end to something that was once there, fear, insecurity, and a failure mentality.

Let me insert here the words of Paul when he said, *"Not that I have already attained, or am already perfected; but I press on, that I may lay hold of that for which Christ Jesus has also laid hold of me"* (Philippians 3:12). Paul was saying that he had not become everything he wanted to be as a Christian. He was not finished yet, but was determined to pursue the goal before him. Paul's focus had been redefined.

The prize was in sight and it was full speed ahead. Being yielded to the Lord is much the same way. It has a way of redirecting your focus to the right things, namely Jesus and His plans and purposes. It magnifies Him in such a way, that you yourself cannot take the credit.

Having been enabled to yield to the Lord in this way, brought more demonstration of the Spirit's power. Being able to give way to the Holy Spirit is having confidence in *His* ability. Being yielded is the discovery that Someone bigger, mightier, and greater lives in you! Once discovered, you want to let Him out!

Our identity is realized when we know by experience who it is living in us! Jesus said to the woman at the well, *"If you knew the gift of God, and who it is who says to you, 'Give me a drink,' you would have asked Him, and He would have given you living water"* (John 4:10). I know Jesus is talking about eternal life. He said it to me this way, "Gloria, if you knew the gift of God in you, you would ask, and I would give." Everything we do is for the purpose of giving life. The Lord uses our willingness to yield to Him to bring life to people in a variety of ways. One of those ways is through preaching. The gospel of Jesus Christ is the power of God bringing salvation. Another way Jesus brings life is through the gifts of the Holy Spirit. Paul told the church at Corinth that he came to them with the testimony of God (1 Corinthians 2:1). Jesus was the central theme of his preaching. The Holy Spirit testified that the message

Paul preached was true by working with him through demonstrations of the Spirit's power.

What was the reason? So that people would put their trust in God rather than the wisdom of man. The Amplified Bible states in 1 Corinthians 2:2 that Paul resolved to know nothing, to be *"conscious"* of nothing except Jesus Christ. This is what it means to be yielded, conscious of nothing else but Jesus!

A Testimony of Accomplishment

These testimonies are being shared that Jesus might be glorified. I know that I am nothing without Him. After a lifetime of training, I was finally seeing those things I had longed to see come to pass. When we discover our true born-again identity, and the One who really lives in us, we will uncover the plans and purposes of God. We will know who we truly are in Christ Jesus. Therefore, a desire comes to walk worthy of the One who lives in us; to fully please Him and finish the work He has uncovered for us to do.

One of the first notable things that took place after my disappearing act happened in Kampala, Uganda, East Africa. I had just preached the morning session. We offered prayer for the sick and needy. As I was exiting the building, a pastor stopped me. He said, "Pastor Gloria this man has come for prayer. He has heard in the city that there is a lady from the United States that believes her God can heal the sick." He further explained to me that he was a Muslim with tuberculosis. The doctors had done all they could.

He was not getting better. He then spoke some challenging words to me: "If your God can heal me, I will serve Him." Oh my goodness, something rose up in me! It was the Holy Spirit. Speaking by the Holy Ghost, with my finger pointing in his face, I said, "My God is going to heal you because He is not dead but alive!" I had never spoken with such force or boldness. I knew that I knew, that I knew, God was going to heal that man. I prayed a very simple prayer and went to lunch.

Later that day, the pastor came to get me for the evening service. His voice was dancing with excitement. He shared with me that the man never left the building. He supposed that he had gotten saved. I asked if someone prayed with him and the pastor said he did not think so. I replied, "Then he is not saved." That night when I gave the altar call, this man Hussein, came forward. I asked him if he wanted to be saved. He answered, "Yes." With broken English, this man confessed Jesus Christ as his Lord and Savior. The complete understanding of all that had taken place did not become known until the next morning. Hussein showed up for the meeting. The pastor became ecstatic while pointing at him. He took the platform and asked Hussein if he would testify. He testified that he had come the day before feeling very ill. After receiving prayer, he knew that something happened. He knew he had experienced healing and as a result he gave his heart to Jesus the night before. The reason the pastor was so excited was because Hussein came in completely shaven. When asked about his clean shaven face, he cheerfully declared, "I am no longer a

Muslim. I am a Christian." I am telling you the truth; I literally witnessed a transformation in this man's countenance. Darkness became light. He was smiling from ear to ear aglow with the light and life of the Spirit of God!

Six months later, the pastor from Uganda came to my church. He shared how Hussein had to leave the country because of death threats upon his life. He is now preaching the gospel of Jesus Christ. This is humanly impossible, but God did it!

Accomplishment takes place when we know who lives in us. There are works the Lord has planned just for you. I can not explain to you the joy that comes from walking along side the Lord in accomplishing His will.

More Proof

Time will not permit me to speak of all the marvelous things I have witnessed. There was an 89 year old man who was deaf in one ear who is no longer deaf. In one single service in the bush of Kenya, Africa, 20 people were instantly healed of hernias. They would poke and feel themselves asking where it had gone. My answer, "I don't know!"

Another pastor from Kalerwe, Uganda had asked me to preach in his church. After preaching the word, an altar call was given. A woman came up for prayer who had been hemorrhaging. She had been hemorrhaging for weeks. She was growing very weak. Her husband was insisting she go to the doctor. She said she was waiting for the revival meetings to start at the church. She made her way to the meeting that night. We would not know what took place until Sunday. She was near death and her family was still insisting that she get medical treatment. She told them to get her to church that the Lord would heal her there. After prayer and before she reached home that night her bleeding had completely stopped and she was shouting the victory.

I can't begin to tell the testimonies of how the Lord has set people free from evil spirits. I have seen them come out screaming. I have watched people fall limp to the ground after being delivered. I have seen them bow down and worship the Lord in humble thanksgiving and devotion.

There's also the gifts of the Holy Spirit, especially the gift of the word of knowledge that comes to expose sin, sickness, and bondage from the past. At other times, it will reveal certain facts about a person that many times no one else knows. God is letting them know He knows all about them. It is indescribable. It is awesome. It is supernatural. It is the Holy Ghost.

I share these things with you to encourage you that your dreams can and will be realized. Do not give up. If God has made a promise to you, He will see to it that it comes to pass. Remember He is unable to lie. Abraham received a promise. He patiently endured, and later, he obtained the promise (Hebrews 6:15). It may not come in a month, a year, or even ten years, but God is faithful and He will do it! The book of Hebrews records Sarah's testimony of faith. "*By faith Sarah herself also received strength to conceive seed, and she bore a child when she was past the age, because she judged Him faithful who had promised"* (11:11).

You have been born-again to work for and serve the Lord. It is His will that you accomplish everything He has planned for your life. May you, like Paul, be able to say at the end of your life, *"I have fought the good fight, I have finished the race, I have kept the faith. Finally, there is laid up for me the crown of righteous-ness, which the Lord, the righteous Judge, will give to me on that Day, and not to me only but also to all who have loved His appearing"* (2 Timothy 4:7-8).

> *For in Him dwells all the fullness of the*
> *Godhead bodily, and you are*
> *complete in Him, who is the head of all*
> *principality and power.*
> Colossians 2:9-10

Chapter 11

Identity in Christ Alone

In the beginning of this book, I shared about my first encounter with identity reshaping. It began when the Lord asked me to step down from leading the women's ministry. This was a very painful process. From this position, I then became credentialed with the Assemblies of God. My pastor gave me a staff position; my job description would be pastor of evangelism and discipleship. It included teaching a Sunday school class to new believers, and having the opportunity to preach once a month.

What I thought was a demotion ended up being a spiritual promotion. I was enjoying this new phase of ministry along with the new responsibilities. Two years later, the Lord began to deal with my heart to resign.

I felt He was calling me to evangelistic ministry. I argued that it would be a whole lot easier to step down if I had somewhere to go. The Lord responded by letting me know if I would step down *then* I would have doors open to me. He was right. I have found that all these adjustments have a lot to do with obedience. God always blesses obedience. Doors began to open for me and I was having a lot of fun. The more I was gone though, the more I felt like a stranger at my home church. It wasn't my pastor's fault. It was not really anyone's fault. It was something the Lord was doing. The winds of change were blowing my way and I did not know where they were leading me.

The Winds of Change

After being gone a couple of weeks, I was back attending my home church. Pastor John and I had a system by which we would communicate. He had asked me if I had anything from the Lord. I let him know that I did and he welcomed me to the pulpit.

I shared from Isaiah six. It was the part where he saw the Lord high and lifted up in His rightful place, above everything else. I exhorted the congregation that the Lord was calling us to a deeper surrender in worship. It isn't my intention to sound redundant, but once again, I was not expecting what was to happen next. A lady stood up and with her hand on her hip she retorted, "I am sick and tired of coming to church to get beat up." I slithered back to my seat and let my pastor handle the situation. He was always so good at handling things like that. It seemed he had to many times where I was concerned due to the fact that many people misunderstood my passion.

"What did I do wrong, Lord?" I did not understand how she took that the wrong way. I knelt down on my knees and began to intercede. The Lord spoke to my heart that I was not being received. Once again, I was crushed. He also told me it was time to shake the dust off my feet. This was not said to me to be negative, but necessary. I did not want to hear it. This was my home church. I thought I would be there until Jesus came back. I realize now, that the Lord was calling me to begin to spread my wings and fly. I had to let go of what was so that I could embrace what was to be. This was a very traumatic time for me. What was the Lord trying to do to me, kill me? The answer was yes. He was trying to kill my desires. It was here in this place that I realized that my identity crisis was not getting fixed it was just taking on new positions and titles. The Lord was calling me to leave, but where was I to go?

A Wilderness Experience

The next couple of years would be extremely painful for me. I was lost and it seemed no one knew how to find me, including me. I questioned my motives time and time again. I wondered if I had made the right decisions. There was nothing but silence.

One day while digging a trench in my yard, the Lord broke the silence. He spoke to my heart and said, "I have brought you to this wilderness place for My purposes. I am Lord over the wilderness." Thank God! Finally, He had spoken. I still did not know much, but I knew God was in control. There was a lot of healing that had to take place in my life. I had to work through many hurtful emotions. It seemed like an eternity of barrenness. I wanted so badly for it to be over. I did not recognize it at the time, but the Lord was taking me through another long process of identity reshaping.

In this desolate place, I was all alone. No one could be there with me. There was nothing going on around me. I became so desperate for the Lord. I yearned to have a word from Him. I longed to understand His purpose and know His will. Even though I knew God had a plan for my life, it seemed He too, had forgotten me. The one thing that brought me relief and comfort was remembering the great men of God who also had wilderness experiences. I thought about how David tended sheep. He was called to be a king, yet there he was in a far away place from a palace. It paid off though. He had a lion and bear experience that prepared him for the day he would confront Goliath. No one knew it, but David was getting to know the Lord privately and intimately.

We have to mention Moses. He too had a wilderness experience. He actually had two of them. The first one took place before he led the children of Israel out of Egypt. He had some personal conflicts to resolve. He exhausted all his excuses. Perhaps he thought he had blown it so badly that God was punishing him. He too knew years of silence. The Lord did break the silence when He spoke from the burning bush. His next wilderness experience would not be alone; it would be with millions of people.

There were still more obstacles to overcome. Moses had learned to trust God. His developed trust would save him time and again.

We will have wilderness experiences also. I do not like them very much, but looking back over my life, I see their importance. Some things can't come any other way, they just can't. Believe me; God knows exactly where you are because He placed you there. He orchestrates everything from the beginning to the end. He will come at just the right time and break the silence. Wait patiently for Him.

My First Pastorate

I tried to find my identity in so many things up to this point; women's ministry director, teacher, pastor of evangelism and discipleship, church member, credentialed minister, and even evangelist. Slowly, there came a turn on the Wilderness Road. I was being invited to minister more and more and was having a lot of fun.

In the midst of all this fun, I received a call from my presbyter. The pastor of the Huntingburg church had resigned. I was sure he wanted me to fill in. I was willing until they found someone. The presbyter did not want me to just fill in he wanted me to become the new pastor. "No," was my reply. I was not interested in being the pastor of a church. I was having too much fun traveling. My presbyter responded, "You have not even prayed about it." I explained to him that I did not need to, neither did I want to. He asked me if I would at least pray about it. I agreed.

I went into prayer for about five minutes. Basically, I assumed the Lord was in agreement with me about this. I thanked Him for understanding. A few days later I was traveling to a city about an hour away for a meeting. I was sensing the Lord was drawing me into prayer. I spent more than three hours praying in the Holy Ghost that day. I did not like what I was hearing.

You know I became the pastor of that church, don't you? Once again, I was being asked to do something I really did not want to be doing. It was a totally different vein of ministry. I had witnessed the struggles and hurts of being a pastor. I did not want anything to do with it. I felt like I had been called to the back side of the desert, and I had more excuses than Moses did. I had a few conflicts too. I grew up in this town. No one would take me seriously. Besides that, I was sure there were a thousand others better qualified than me. Being a pastor was not on my list of things to do, especially when it came to my identity. You see there were only a handful of people there. My first Sunday, we had 12 in attendance. The previous pastor was there to introduce me to the congregation, his wife, my family and me, along with five other members. Two of them left after the first Sunday. My thoughts were, "You have got to be kidding Lord." He was not kidding at all. He was very serious. It was not so bad at first, but it began to take a toll on me.

There was absolutely no commitment. Classrooms would sit empty because teachers would not show up for their class. Finances were low. The building needed a new roof. The women's bathroom needed a new floor. The wooden doors were rotting and the windows had been targets for BB gun practice. There was no cleaning lady, secretary, and there wasn't even a phone in the office. I felt like I had been dropped off in the wilderness again. I did not know how to deal with it, and I became angry at the Lord. I was bored and found no satisfaction or fulfillment. In my heart, I still wanted to travel. Frustration was welling up inside me which eventually turned into rebellion. The saddest part of all, I was too blind to see it.

A Rebellious Heart

Throughout this book, I have continually made reference to certain people in my life. Once again, I would like to communicate that this is not about the individuals I speak of, but to share about the work the Lord would do in me. Along with the frustration and anger of the church situation, there was also a certain relationship I found to be very controlling. This person became a shadow in my life. Quit frankly, I did not handle it very well at all. Resentment toward this person began to grow in me. I felt as if I were being smothered. Everything I did, she wanted to do it too. Anything I bought, she had to buy an identical one. Everywhere my family went, she thought she had to go also. It was becoming unbearable. I just wanted my life back! No one seemed to hear me. It was as if no one was listening to me, especially my husband.

This woman was very needy. There were tremendous fears and insecurities; rejection was a deep root and she feared being alone. I felt as if a tick had attached itself to me and was draining the life out of me. This is the best way to describe it. Please understand this is not to slander the woman, there was a demonic spirit behind it. At the same time, she was quit efficient. She became my secretary, but she did not stay within the boundaries. She would get to the office hours before I did and finish all my work. This was not something I had asked her to do. She was assuming this role. When I would confront her, she would say it was her way of letting me know how much she loved and appreciated me. She began to tell people things that were not completely true. Once while I was away in Africa, she signed my name on some papers as if she were me. Another lady in the church questioned her about it and she told her that I had given her permission to do it, but I had only given her the right to sign her name with the words "for Gloria Kramer."

This woman would show up at my house six days a week. I had no privacy. She was literally assuming my identity. She was trying to step in and parent my children. She once answered my phone as my personal maid. You may be asking why I put up with all of it, but a lot of it I didn't know until much later. I trusted her and had no reason to ask questions. Please hear me, one lesson I have learned, always ask a lot of questions! An image had been created before other people that kept them from asking questions of their own. She placed herself as a fortress around my life that kept people from having access to me. It was not spoken with words, but it was silently communicated. I really believe she was unaware that she was participating in a demonic scheme from hell. Inside however, my spirit was agitated. It was as if the Lord would say things to me about the situation, but my emotions could not receive it. She would always say flattering things to me. She called me a mighty woman of God. She would tell me if she could be like anyone, she would be like me. I would always tell her she needed to be like Jesus. She told me many times that she was my armor bearer (like Jonathan was to David) and that she would die for me. I questioned how the things I was sensing about her could be true when she would say things like that to me? I can tell you now; it was the influence of an evil spirit.

Believe me; I took this to the Lord many, many times in prayer. I found the resentment and pressure of it all was burying me alive. I wanted to be free! I became consumed with it. My thoughts turned inward. Inside I was screaming, "What about me? What about what I want? Does anyone care?" I might add here, this is a very dangerous place to be! Jesus said He did not come to be served, but to serve, and give His life a ransom for many (Mark 10:45). Death lurks in the shadows of our life when we move from this focus. I began to run from it all. My husband and I had many arguments concerning this woman. He always thought I was too hard on her. He was not hearing my heart. He was not listening to my pain; instead he was defending this woman and not me, his own wife. Time and time again, I would try to talk to him about her, but my complaints fell on deaf ears. I began to shut the doors to my heart. I was tired of being hurt. I was tired of trying to get him to hear me. If he didn't care, then neither would I, was my response. This is a rebellious heart.

A Biblical Answer

Rebellion develops in the *unwilling* heart. In 1 Samuel 15, Samuel anoints Saul to be king. He then is commanded to heed the voice of the Lord. His assignment was to utterly destroy the Amalekites. In verse nine, Saul spares king Agag and the best of all that was good. The Bible says he was *unwilling* to completely destroy them. The reasons could be many and varied. Maybe he wanted prestige and honor by flaunting the good spoil. Or, perhaps, he was simply being selfish. Whatever the case, he was only interested in pursuing his own desires rather than serving the Lord. The most heart wrenching part of this story is the Lord's response in verse 11, " '*I greatly regret that I have set up Saul as king, for he has turned back from following Me, and has not performed My commandments.' And it grieved Samuel, and he cried out to the Lord all night.*"

Samuel is sent to meet with Saul. Saul gleefully announces to Samuel that he finished his assignment. Notice that was not God's evaluation of the situation. Samuel answers, "Really? Then why do I hear sheep and oxen in the background?" Rebellion turns to deception when responsibility is not accepted. Saul blames the people for his actions. *They* wanted to do it. Not only that, he justifies it all by acknowledging it was done for the Lord. It was all lies and deception. Saul was lying to himself. He was lying to Samuel. More importantly, he was lying to God. Saul was given another chance. Instead of admitting his rebellious attitude and disobedient actions, he maintained his innocence (v. 20). This is where it really gets serious. Let's look at the following verses together.

> *So Samuel said: "Has the Lord as great delight in burnt offerings and sacrifices, as in obeying the voice of the Lord? Behold, to obey is better than sacrifice, and to heed than the fat of rams. For rebellion is as the sin of witchcraft, and stubbornness is as iniquity and idolatry. Because you have rejected the word of the Lord, He also has rejected you from being king."*
>
> (1 Samuel 15:22-23)

Samuel conveyed to Saul just how serious it was. Obedience, sincerity, and honesty are the right requirements for the kind of worship that pleases God. Saul's attitude and actions were denying the Lord's authority. This was just as critical as the willful defiance Satan shows toward God's authority through the power of witchcraft. Saul acted independently of the Lord. He was blatantly stubborn. He wanted what he desired more than he wanted to please God. This was, in essence, the sin of idolatry because he elevated his will above God's (The Nelson Study Bible, p. 476).

I am sorry to say, I was also guilty of the same things. I wanted to blame this woman. I wanted to blame being at the church. I wanted to blame my husband for not caring enough to defend me. I wanted to blame God. After all, if I had not taken the position of pastor, I would not be in this rebellious mess. Wrong! I had to take responsibility for my actions. Even if all these things were true, Biblically, I had no right to respond this way. When I realized the seriousness of my actions, I was devastated! I was also repentant.

Rebellion will bring death. It brought death to Saul's life. He was rejected by the Lord from being His representative. Death came to many areas of my life as well.

Lost Consciousness

In the last chapter, I spoke about how being yielded was necessary to accomplish God's plans and purposes. I had allowed many weeds to grow in my life. My ability to yield was being strangled by stubbornness and rebellion. What happened? How did I get away from the Shekinah glory of God? In a word, sin.

I had wanted to live in that place of being yielded. I liked losing all consciousness of me. It was as if I were truly connected to the Lord; a closeness I desired with Him had been realized. How did I get back there? I was now unproductive due to distraction. That night in Jamaica, one thing was certain; I had touched a new realm. It was unknown territory. It was un-chartered waters, but I really liked it and I wanted it back. I knew there was more, and yet I lost my focus. Lost consciousness of God became stupidity. That special endowment had brought a new closeness, but it also began a new battle, only I did not know it at the time. I found myself blind-sided. I had allowed myself to become unguarded and unprotected. After all the lessons, all the waiting time, and all the hardships already overcome, you would think I would have been smarter. I lost consciousness of the Lord . . . again!

D-Day!

This would take a toll on my family and especially my marriage. To be honest, my hard heart had developed an "I don't care attitude." I stopped fighting for all the things that mattered. Sin is like cancer, it spreads. It contaminates everything and everyone it touches. The end result is death. My husband filed for a divorce, and three years later, after twenty-four years of marriage, he divorced me. This was the most devastating thing I have ever walked through. I went through so many emotions. I experienced anger and rejection that went so deep; I nearly had a nervous breakdown. Thank God for the ability to pray in other tongues. I would not be here today without that wonderful gift! After all the titles, positions, and countless identity crises', I thought the one thing I could count on was being a wife. Once again, I did not know who I was. In every title I had placed my confidence I found emptiness, heartache, and pain. I honestly did not know how to continue.

I begged the Lord to release me from the church and offered my resignation. I hand delivered every reason He needed to let me go. Men came to me with their Bibles open explaining why I needed to step down from my position. After all, the Bible does say that if you can not run your own house, you have no business running the church, doesn't it? (See 1Timothy 3:4). It was so tempting to get a one way ticket to anywhere! I wanted to go where no one knew my name. I was open to any relocation program, but none came. I would have to walk this out just like everything else. A dear friend, an evangelist, came to see me. After talking, he prayed this prayer "Lord, I thank you that Gloria will be a better wife, a better mother, and a better minister having gone through this." What? Did he not hear me? I was facing divorce. That was it, all the support and encouragement he could offer? Did he not know how much I was hurting? I was offended and angry with that prayer at the time. Thank you, Brother Charles, for praying that prayer. I have grown to be a better person. I did for a time grow bitter, but with God's help, I have chosen to be better.

It has been a long process filled with many tears and a lot of pain. If I wanted to experience healing, I had to open my heart and let Him come in. Just as Adam and Eve hid from the presence of the Lord, I was hiding too. Where can you flee from the presence of the Lord? He is everywhere (see Psalm

139). Just as He conversed with Adam and Eve, He continued to converse with me. He did not yell and scream at me. Instead, He brought forgiveness and hope. He consistently encouraged me to get back up. How Lord? "With My help," was always His reply. I love Him so much! I truly owe Him my life. My wings had been broken and crushed, but He gave me new wings so I could fly again. I never realized the type of death divorce could bring, but I have found in Jesus, resurrection is possible. Joy can be found in obediently serving Him.

By the way, I have enjoyed being a pastor more than I thought I could. It is where the Lord placed me and I want to be where He wants me to be.

Go Forward

Those powerful words were coming to me again, "You can not go forward looking backward." I knew that, but this time was different. I did not want to go forward. I wanted to wallow in self pity and die. Jesus, however, reaches into tombs of death in order to bring resurrection. He is alive! Because He lives, I do too, and you can also.

My mind went through months of agonizing torment. I could not eat or sleep. Just like those ten spies, I was looking at the wrong things. I was not only looking at the wrong things, I was meditating on the wrong things. I knew where the rewind button was. I kept pushing it, and it kept the wound open. I had a choice to make. This thought plagued me most, "Who will want a divorced woman with three children living at home to stand in their pulpit?" Everything seemed lost. I feared that the ugly d-word would handicap my ministry as well. It was all I knew. It was all I felt like I had left. It is important to insert here that the most important aspect in all of this was my relationship with Jesus. I began to understand that it wasn't about marriage, titles, position, not even a ministry; it was about being in right standing with Him.

To be called a child of God is the most endearing title of all! When it is all said and done, my relationship with Jesus is the only thing that will last. The good news, out of my relationship with Him, I discovered He still had use of me. I was able to get up knowing that God, who is the Alpha and Omega, knew all of this would happen. Yet, He called and chose me anyway! He would say, "Gloria, I am *your* beginning and end. I know every turn in your road, every bend. I have already walked ahead of you. Now, go forward!"

I preach today not because I love the ministry (although I do). No. I preach because I love Jesus. We serve a mighty, able, awesome God! When we are faithless, He remains faithful!

We Wrestle With Principalities

The words uttered by the evil spirit that vomited in my room many years earlier, began to come back to my remembrance. Those words, "I am going to kill the messenger," the ones I did not take seriously were proving to be quit accurate. At times, I felt like

I was dying. The rebellion and divorce seemed to bring me close to death . . . but God!

Those words from the Apostle Paul in Ephesians 6:12 had a whole new meaning. *"For we do not wrestle against flesh and blood, but against principalities, against powers, against the rulers of the darkness of this age, against spiritual hosts of wickedness in the heavenly places."* They are written for a reason. We would be wise to heed them!

It is the devil who brings destruction with the intended purpose of stealing and destroying the life of God. Jesus came to combat that strategy by giving us His life so that we could experience true life in abundance.

All the people in my life who opposed me, all the hurtful things they did and said to me, they were not the enemy. The Lord was showing me it had all been brought about with the intention to abort the plans and purposes of God. I honestly did not see myself as a threat to the enemy. This was part of the problem. We are a threat to the enemy, not because of our greatness, but due to the fact the Greater One lives in us! When we can genuinely take hold of this truth, we will rise up in the power of the Spirit and turn cities upside down! When we can truly understand that our source of life comes from the life of Another, we will experience His supernatural dynamics.

Let me leave you with this thought. In Acts 13:8 some very interesting things are disclosed. *"But Elymas the sorcerer (for so his name is translated) withstood them, seeking to turn the proconsul away from the faith."* Paul and Barnabas had been called and commissioned. They were sent out by the Holy Spirit. This proconsul had invited them to come and preach the Word of God but this sorcerer got in the way. He had a deliberate assignment to turn the proconsul away from faith in Jesus Christ, but it did not work! There are deceitful assignments from the enemy of righteousness who continually tries to pervert the ways of the Lord (see verse ten). He is the true agent behind any person he may be using. Do not underestimate him. He is a liar, and the truth is not in him.

Beauty for Ashes

Beauty for ashes, this is the promise of God. Jesus came to give us beauty for ashes, the oil of joy for mourning, the garment of praise for the spirit of heaviness, so that we could be called the trees of righteousness, the planting of the Lord (Isaiah 61:3). What was the Lord's purpose? So that He would be glorified. That is so awesome!

Recently, I was invited to travel to Israel and minister. I was elated with joy. This had been a dream of mine for many years. I would have been happy to go as a tourist, but to get to go and also preach . . . well that was a touch of heaven on earth.

I had met this couple from Louisiana at a Flame Convention where we were all invited as guest speakers. We hit it off and went to dinner after the meeting. We talked (I did most of it) for hours. They asked me if I would like to go to Israel with them sometime. I immediately said yes.

Several months later when it came time to leave, we flew separate flights and they were delayed in New York. I am sitting in Israel with this host couple I have never met and the first question they ask, "How does your husband feel about you traveling?" Oh no! I had only been there a few hours. My response, "He is backslidden and I would appreciate it if you would pray for him." Later that night, back in my room, the Holy Spirit got a hold of me. He drilled me, "You were not completely honest with them."

"But Lord? Do they have to know every skeleton in my closet within the first few hours I arrive?" It was another night of wrestling, and I lost again! The Lord showed me my heart. He unraveled my fears one thread at a time. He was revealing the same heart of fear I had so many years earlier with the evangelist friend. Here we go again. He let me see how afraid I really was. "You are afraid if they know the truth about your marital status, they won't receive you." That would be correct. It was a constant nagging question. Would they welcome my ministry? I knew in my heart I had to tell them the truth.

It went surprisingly well. It was not a hindrance at all. Thank you Lord, but this was only one person. At the first meeting, Dan got up to introduce me. I want him to know that one of the things he said that day released me to write this book. He said, "From the first time we met this lady and heard her speak, we knew she had authority in the Spirit." In the midst of all the *stuff*, there was still evidence that God was at work in my life. I am so thankful to Jesus.

Days later, I was talking with one of the women pastors. I was staying in her home. She commented about a word I had given her. She was relaying to me that it was right on and that she knew what it meant. Her compliment to me was that she recognized I heard from the Lord. The next thing she would say was also instrumental in my being released to write this book. She told me how she was talking to the Lord about it. This is what He said to her, "She has paid a price for it." Thank you Lord for not giving up on me!

In each church I was privileged to preach, I was introduced with warm words of respect and honor. I was not there as a married woman, or a single woman. I was there as a servant of the Lord; that is the reason they received me.

I was also privileged to speak at a Women's Conference. I did not even know we were doing a women's conference before leaving the states. The Lord spoke to my heart to tell them of the hurtful last years of my life. He promised me, "If you will obey Me, I will deliver them from their pain of yesterday and bring them into healing today." I stood in awe at the presence of the Lord. I did not have to do anything. He just moved in and began to reach into the depths of their hearts. Women were kneeling totally surrendered to the love of God. Tears were flowing down their faces as the Lord ushered in His gentle healing touch. The very thing I wanted to hide from these precious people was one of the reasons the Lord had sent me. Who can fathom that? It is only possible because of Jesus. He deserves the glory and the honor!

Identity in Christ Alone

It is my sincerest desire that something I have shared in these pages will minister to you. Whether you are male or female, young or old, we have all struggled to find our identity. I have learned that these truths have been used time and time again. The faces of the trials change, but the truth of God's Word stands. I am not implying that my identity reshaping is complete. I am sure it is not complete. It is my prayer that these pages offer an arsenal of weaponry to help you overcome the enemy and enable you to take back your born-again identity! May you find relevance for your own life and discover that God has created you for His purpose. It is not what you do, or the title you hold or don't hold, it is who you really *know*!

Knowing Jesus is the first step in finding your born-again identity. He truly desires for you to discover that He is the greater One living within you. He wants you to become more conscious of Him every day you live. This discovery ensures that you will successfully realize your destiny.

Things happen in life we can't always prepare for, but we have the testimonies of the "great cloud of witnesses" in Hebrews chapter 11. These saints overcame violence, torture, imprisonment, and even death because of their faith and trust in the Lord (11:32-40). Because of the conscious awareness of

Jesus who lives in me, I have found the ability to *"lay aside every weight, and the sin which so easily ensnares us, and let us run with endurance the race that is set before us, looking unto Jesus, the author and finisher of our faith. . ."* (Hebrews 12:1-2). Weight is anything that hinders or keeps you pinned down. I had to throw aside the weight of divorce, rejection, and pain so that I could rediscover the power of the One who lives in me and get back into the race.

I love life! I am again enjoying my life. I am learning to refocus my attention on the fact that my identity is in Christ, rather than in the facts of divorce. We are told that God knows the plans He has made for us. They are plans for good and include a bright future. No matter the scenery, He promises to be by our side. We are only given one chance to live. Each of us are called to live it to the fullest; to make the most of every opportunity. Life is far too short to hold grudges or waste time on things that we are powerless to change. Remember, "Where you are, is not where you are going. Where you have been, is not where you have to stay!"

*For [as far as this world is concerned] you
have died,
and your [new, real] life is hidden with
Christ in God.*
Colossians 3:3, Amplified

If you prayed the prayer leading to salvation in chapter six, please write and let us know. We would love to hear from you. Write to:

Called Out Ministries, Inc.
215 South Washington Street
Huntingburg, IN 47542

Or you can email us at calloutm@fullnet.com

To order additional copies of the book or for speaking engagements, you may also contact the above address.

About the Author

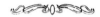

Rev. Gloria Kramer has a heart for souls, a passion to see the body of Christ fulfill their God given destinies, and a determination to take Jesus to the nations. The hand of the Lord is evident upon her life as she operates under a heavy anointing with an "unshakable" faith and devotion to do the work of the ministry.

Gloria ministers with great grace and zeal and the Lord uses her mightily. She always ministers with fervent expectancy and the Lord always moves. Her conviction is commanding, her preaching uncompromising and her desire to serve Jesus is consuming.

The proud mother of a son, Tony (his wife Kristy), and three daughters Cheryl, Elisha, and Kendra, and one grandson Caleb, she resides in Indiana. Gloria currently pastors a church and continues to travel the globe as a prophetic voice with a passion to make Jesus real!

Printed in the United States
55696LVS00002B/145-306